JEAN-MICHEL OUGHOURLIAN

with Maryse VENDRE and Jean-Marc RICHARD

WORK THAT HEALS

The individual,
the organization,
the society

TABLE OF CONTENTS

FOREWORD

I undertook to write this book following my visits to the various learning factories founded and managed by AMIPI which employ people with cognitive disabilities. The result is a field study reporting on the experience lived by a psychiatrist in the light of mimetic psychology.

This experience has shown me, once again, the effectiveness of a learning system that throws students into a swimming pool to teach them how to swim rather than lecturing in front of a blackboard or on a gymnastic mat. The foundation of this learning method is based on old popular wisdom: practice makes perfect.

I would like to express my sincere appreciation to the founder and chairman of AMIPI - Mrs. Maryse Vendre, and Mr. Jean-Marc Richard - who generously contributed to the writing of this book.

Jean-Michel Oughourlian

PREFACE

MODEL
By Jean-Marc Richard
President of the AMIPI Foundation, Member of the
College of Founders

*To Maurice Vendre who made me discover the virtues and
merits of "Homo Faber".*
*To Jean-Michel Oughourlian who showed me the
significance of our research and programs in overcoming the
violence that is specific to rivalry".*
To all the "sapiens friends" called the "amipiens"

This book is full of perspectives that reveal how to learn
and how to transmit knowledge.

We can start reading it by opening the afterword by
Maryse Vendre where we find the story of her career and that
of AMIPI, the medico-pedagogical institute that she co-
founded with Maurice Vendre in the 1960s. Thanks to a
special learning concept based on the plasticity of the brain,
this institute was later converted into six learning and
inclusive factories, in which most of the employees are

suffering from often severe cognitive disabilities. Yet as employees, they are producing high-tech products – cable harnesses for cars - 8 million a year for customers such as Stellantis, Renault, Flex-n-Gate, Plastic Omnium, among others.

These customers view their cooperation with AMIPI as supporting "a collective intelligence which represents the synthesis of the liberal economy's best attributes: providing people suffering from a cognitive handicap with the opportunity to work, to develop themselves and to bloom, while simultaneously affording some economic relief for the state in the realm of public expenditures". I quote here Jean-Dominique Senard, CEO of Renault and one initiator of the French PACT Law, when he refers to AMIPI and the commitments that his group has made as part of its corporate social and environmental responsibility.

We can also read this book by directly immersing ourselves in these factories, guided by Professor Jean-Michel Oughourlian, a noted neuropsychiatrist. During his first visit he clearly stated: "At my place (the hospital), they would become vegetables!". He was talking about his psychiatric service where those with cognitive disabilities are regarded as "sick" patients. A statement I cannot forget.

Finally, we can start reading this book by focusing on the theoretical base discussed with Professor Oughourlian, examining the implementation methods of his mimetic psychology and how it is put into practice in our organization. Put more simply, it is about getting colleagues to become role models for others.

In 2005, at the age of 45, having been a volunteer administrator for 20 years, I was appointed volunteer chairman of AMIPI by Maurice and Maryse Vendre. This institution is known as AMIPI-Bernard Vendre and is recognized as a public utility Foundation. My only prior experience was that of a successful salesperson, justifying an extensive knowledge of economics, acquired at the Essec business school in Paris. Besides a strong curiosity, a sense of organization, and anticipation.

Still, did these credentials entitle me to become the President of an industrial and scientific organization? I then asked myself some basic questions that contributed to clearing my thoughts and determining my actions. How do we learn? How can we safeguard the future of these factories in light of the financial globalization phenomenon, which has generated a delocalization of the main power from Europe toward countries where the average monthly salary, employer taxes included, is below 300 euros?

Despite all the challenges, we kept progressing, and we grew. The AMIPI is now composed of 900 employees (750 of whom are suffering from cognitive disorders) and 150 supervisors. They are all fond of the well-done job and possess a sense of curiosity, observation and research. It is above all a dual-mission organization - both industrial and scientific - a unique place where we can experience the plasticity of the brain, and where the insights of great scientists such as Professors Marie-Claude Potier, Pamela Banta-Lavenex, Pascale Toscani, and others are regularly solicited.

On-site, we help them identify various avenues of research and carry out in-depth studies over long periods. These research studies not only to publications but also to the development of protocols for our six learning and inclusive factories. The success of this method is evidenced when our operators, once they have gained self-confidence and autonomy, leave us to integrate into a general working environment. Some 20 to 40 operators make this transition each year. Fortunately, very few fail.

AMIPI is becoming today a place of experiment, oriented toward ministries such as those of Industry, Labor, Health, and, of course, it has made the inclusion of these people a major high stake challenge. AMIPI is also a place referred to by different french administrations such as the General Directorate for Employment and Vocational Training (DGEFP), and organizations as important as Agefiph (Association for the management of funds for the professional integration of disabled people).

Some little-known facts are very significant – for example, the overall cost of work is four times lower than the cost of non-work. This situation can be quite profitable to the State: a person who does not work costs society 30,000 euros per year.

We succeed every day in showing the influence of work on the brain, but not just any work. While repetitive tasks can lead to deterioration, the opposite is true: continuous learning as we have conceived and practiced them, help the brain to develop further.

My encounter with Professor Jean-Michel Oughourlian, initially through the reading and analysis of his various works and research and then in person, has guided us forward.

In his masterpiece "The mimetic Brain"[1], I found the common denominator of our actions in favor of learning and independency; more precisely, the notion of a model expressed in terms of mimetic psychology that the professor has put in place.

The "model" allows us to learn. It requires the following:

- The competencies and skills of each person.

- The intelligence which lies in these competencies, as Maryse Vendre constantly reminds us.

- The desire to transmit. Have fun sticking out your tongue in front of a baby. You will feel within you the desire to be imitated, and it is only then that the baby will in turn stick out his tongue, as if this learning was first linked to your desire to transmit.

- The vigilance regarding poisonous rivalry which, if it spreads, annihilates the learning process because it engages the desire to destroy the interaction, that link with the other through our brains.

In our organization, the popular saying "every man for himself" is not acknowledged and cannot be a universal law. Conversely, we decided to think outside the box and

---

[1] Notre troisième cerveau. La nouvelle révolution psychologique, Albin Michel, 2013.

distinguish ourselves by favoring the emergence of a large number of "learning models" as resources for others. Each one is conscious of his/her responsibility and chooses the models he/her finds useful. As Professor Oughourlian teaches us, brains are disposed in this manner by the "mimetic desire", to learn from the other and then to transmit in turn what was learned. It is the interaction that heals...

The model is quite successful:

700 hirings since 2014.

160 placements in conventional companies in our territories.

On average, 30 million euros of turnover is created each year, which means suppliers can be paid, and our expenditures can be covered.

And more importantly, saving some 20 million euros in public expenditures per year.

This is not a simple matter. Especially in a country where public spending should be more controlled and evaluated thoroughly in order to assess its real impact.

"The brain develops itself by manufacturing", demonstrates Professor Jean-Michel Oughourlian. We could also say that the brain "manufactures" itself by "manufacturing" products. And it extends its developmental capacity by helping not only the individual, but organizations, and the society at large:

1. The individual, because he is no longer regarded as a disabled person.

2. The organization, because it aligns with its business purpose – inclusion and autonomy – which goes beyond the purpose of profit alone.

3. The society at large, because work is a factor of socialization and harmony and acts against the violence that can be committed by a man who is left on his own.

In the end, this model and its development allow us to stand out from the crowd and collectively face our challenging industrial future which is endangered by the effects of globalization with no thought given to the meaning of work and its contribution to people's lives.

The AMIPI, an association for material and intellectual assistance to disabled persons, is more than a conglomerate of factories; it is an organizational model that addresses the human being.

If duly replicated, the model will effectively contribute to healing - not only by helping individuals to develop and become autonomous, but also our organizations and our societies at large.

Long live work, long live freedom, long live the "true" Republic

Jean-Marc Richard

On the 7th of March, 2022, at a time when the guns of violence, peculiar to human beings, thunder in Ukraine.

CHAPTER 1

MIMETIC THEORY, A UNIVERSAL KEY

In 1969, I thought I had learned everything. I had received my medical degree after studying at the Faculty of Strasbourg, and I had just been awarded my degree in neuropsychiatry from the Faculty of Paris. I manipulated the psychotropic molecules that had been recently discovered and that were sufficient to dissipate, or so we wanted to believe, the anxieties and other torments of sick people.

I began my career as a psychiatrist in the Sainte-Anne hospital, in Paris. Then, I quickly understood that I still had a lot to learn. In parallel, I started studying psychology and I attended various seminars conducted by well-known scientists such as Jacques Lacan and Henri Ey. Then, life circumstances led me to René Girard who had just published "Violence and the Sacred"[2]. Girard, whom I consider my mentor, was teaching in the United States and had not yet become famous.

Girard's theory, based on the functioning of human societies through mimetic desire has challenged me. It postulated that every human desire is mimetic and is stirred

---

[2] René Girard, La Violence et le Sacré, Grasset, 1972.

by the desire of the other. Here, he thinks that the strong desire for the same object could create and nourish violence. Later on, we would have multiple opportunities to discuss this theory together. Still, I had already been excited by a hypothesis that was later tested by practice and became a piece of evidence. That theory that I will later suggest calling universal mimesis and that he was applying to anthropology, has also enlightened other different fields, starting with psychology.

In the 4th century before our era, Aristotle noted that "Man is the most "mimetic" of all animals", considering that mimicry is the key to learning. In fact, we are all mimieking, always. We have a natural tendency to imitate from the day of our birth and we continue to do so throughout our entire life.

We imitate when we want to learn how to speak, how to write, how to use a spoon, and later a tool. We also imitate when we behave, we dress in a certain way, or when we want to say hello and thank you in the same language as the opposite person. In short, to become fully human: Because I imitate the others, I build myself as *me*.

What's more, an isolated individual cannot survive. Even though he lives in certain loneliness. Each one of us strives to build himself through his relationship with the other, with all others. This is what René Girard and I have called, *interdividuality* rather than *interindividuality*. For the "me-in-itself", the individual as monomial (meaning "one term" or one measurement) is an illusion. We all know the stories of "wild children", raised by animals and therefore deprived of human mimicry. These "wild children" never find the so-called path of "normality" which includes, for example, speech, social communication, and learning basic things, like using a knife and a fork.

I am not me without the other. I am not, this evening, exactly the same person I was in the morning. The TV show I watched, the newspaper I read, and the discussions I had with my colleagues, and my friends, have necessarily influenced me. Further, the pictures I saw have changed my perception of people, situations, and all my affairs. The mechanisms of mimetism reshape me permanently, and throughout my entire existence I am impacted by specific models we adopt and follow.

It is a method that advertising, commerce, and even industry apply in an intuitive manner, without having clearly formalized it. As a matter of fact, the success of Nespresso is first explained by our desire to imitate George Clooney. It is the same situation for organic or vegetarian food which become popular because famous people have used them. This is the reason we like to imitate celebrities - to act and behave like them, and buy the products they buy.

Mimetism was initially a postulate around which my experience of the human being, within the context of its psychopathological aspects, incited me to create a new metapsychology and psychiatry: the mimetic psychology. Mimetic psychology allowed me not only to explain human mysteries but also to better understand how people's mindset function and to learn how human problems are addressed and how crises and conflicts are resolved. Further, it showed me how the lack of well-being - which can degenerate into neuroses and sometimes into psychoses - is likely to handicap an individual, a group, or a society, leading to some serious and paralyzing dysfunctions.

Advances in neurology, especially those which are related to medical imaging, have confirmed the mimetic theory. This hypothesis was supported by the discovery of the amazing mirror neurons. They were the manifestation, the equivalent of what would have been for Freud the detection by the scanner of the self, the super self, and the unconscious on which he founded his theory.

Those neurons constitute what I call our third brain, next to the first brain, the one of cognition. It is located in the cortex and the second brain, responsible for moods and emotions, also called the limbic system. All three continuously interact. Apprehending and analyzing this interaction, allow us to solve many issues at different levels : the individual issues, the group issues, and more broadly, the issues of the entire society.

The discovery of these mirror neurons was a coincidence: The pizza story. In Parma in 1995, Professor Giacomo Rizzolatti and his team of neuroscientists were studying the brain of a monkey in their laboratory. Later on, during their lunch break, they noticed that the monkey was attentively watching them eating their pizza. At that moment, the monkey's head was covered with sensors linked to a PET scan, a medical imaging process. The aim of the experience was to measure the activity of the brain depending on its absorption of glucose in one or more zones at a given point in time, allowing him to function. Thanks to this device, we can know which areas of the brain are activated to carry out a specific activity such as raising an arm, thinking, remembering, being hungry, feeling pleasure or sorrow, learning something... However, as soon as a guest moved his hand in the pizza's direction, even before touching it, a zone of the monkey's brain specifically linked to the real action of eating was activated without really eating. The brain of the monkey was obviously anticipating the following gesture and was ready to taste the pizza.

Further experiments on humans, using more and more sophisticated PET scans have confirmed the following conclusion: all areas of the brain, including those that control speech or memory, contain neurons that are activated simply because of the determination of others to behave in front of us in a particular way. It is also the case for other neurons located in these areas to react in order to execute an action. If at a table, I see your hand approaching a glass of water, I will drink too. This is because you have awakened my mirror neurons and my desire to imitate you.

These experiments also showed that the activation of the mirror neurons depends on an important factor: Understanding the action that happens in front of us. These neurons will be stimulated if you reach out for that glass of water and I know that you will grab it, then bring it to your lips and quench your thirst. I then spontaneously need a glass of water too. This cannot be possible if I cannot understand the purpose of your gesture and your intention as well, and if there is nothing on the table. These mirror neurons will be more stimulated because of the desire to imitate you for example. The brain of a tennis player who is watching the Roland-Garros tournament will be the scene of an explosion of colors on the PET scan screens. On the other side, nothing will happen in the brain of a person who does not know the rules of the game and who does not want to imitate the moves of the champion. Simply put, he does not feel concerned by the activity itself.

The mirror neurons, and so the mimetic effect grasp the smallest details that allow us to feel the desire, such as the desire to have fun, learn, succeed, and move forward in our life. We know quite well that in psychology, the desire is the movement. If there is no desire, there is no movement; and if there is no movement, there is no desire. The desire is also a means of social cohesion: I would like to look like you and be with you. As an example, I can say that if each morning I dress exactly like you, the same trousers and shirt rather than wearing a Christmas Santa Claus costume, it means that I want to imitate you and be integrated into your group. I learn the same way, speak the same language, adopt the same gestures. I am like others. I want to show my cohesion; therefore, I imitate.

Mirror neurons, as I mentioned before, play a fundamental role in all learning processes. This is because a learning process is based on the imitation of interdividuality. Particularly, it is a continuous movement between brains that connect as if they were working through a Wi-Fi or Bluetooth mode, driven by the desire of others.

This assertion is actually valid for the baby who learns to speak by repeating the words that one pronounces in front of him. It is also true for the child who starts writing by drawing the letters that appear on a piece of paper, as well as for the medical student who performs his internship in the hospital, by observing how his mentor is behaving and/or treating patients, and surely for the apprentice who observes his master and learns to properly hold the tool and use it.

The archetypal model is initially the parent who interacts with his young child. Their relationship is made of continuous imitations and suggestions. The father or the mother shows the way by naturally suggesting the gesture to imitate. Then, the child imitates it to learn how to talk, how to walk, and how to socialize. The model becomes my friend and my companion. I end up developing the same tastes and showing the same attitudes under the effect of suggestions and imitation. Further, it could be the master that I imitate to learn a sport or profession.

When standing in front of my model, I feel that my three brains are interactive. The first one certainly retains the information, but it needs the second to awaken the essential emotion, necessary to facilitate the learning process (I learn much better when I'm ready and happy to learn). Then, in my third brain, the mirror neurons are stimulated. Now and only now, I am ready to imitate my model and he is quite satisfied to see me imitate him and learn what he wants me to learn. We all know that nothing is better than the dialogue and the relationship we strive to build with others over time, intending to learn for example a new language, a new profession, integrate into a new environment, or start working in a new company. We are and/or remain, throughout our lives, apprentices in search of a master or a mentor to mimic and whose desires we imitate.

Still, a question I am often asked in this case: Does mimesis leave room for innovation and, even more, for freedom?

On the one hand, we fortunately have the freedom to choose our model. Therefore, knowing thugs, thieves or lazy people does not necessarily mean that I shall imitate them and become like them.

On the other hand, let's not make the same mistake that Plato did and that was initially considered a point of contention with his disciple Aristotle. Imitation is not the reproduction of the same, a photocopy, or even an exact copy. It is an inspiration. We do believe that true mimetism adds and subtracts information regularly, from what is received from the model. When Leonardo da Vinci painted the Mona Lisa, he obviously lost or neglected some details such as her laugh, smell, the way she walks, etc. However, he adds a lot of other nuances - notably her smile, which still remains across centuries. When a child learns how to draw letters at school, the ones he will end up drawing will look like the model, but they will not be exactly like the original one. He will have his own way of writing. His calligraphic style.

In the same line of thought, following blindly and without thinking is like Panurge's sheep who are all heading for the cliff. They gamble instinctively, imitating each other. Eventually, they will fall into the sea and die. We are in the herd and we act like these sheep. Still, we know that we can also decide freely. Therefore, to escape from this deadly herd, we just need to decide where we will head, and chose not to be unconscious followers. In other words, if we need to imitate in order to move or act, we can always, at least, choose the model we want to imitate and follow. However, the desire which creates the imitation and which is at the base of the learning process is not static. It can evolve.

Because of the load of information provided by the cognitive and emotional brains, and due to the permanent interactions with the brain of the other, the mimetic movement of our third brain oscillates between two contradictory attitudes: the empathy when I consider the other as a model to imitate, or the rejection when this model becomes a rival, even an obstacle, to the accomplishment of my desire and fulfillment of my ambitions.

We thus end up with what I call "the disease of desire": any common approach is blocked. Mirror neurons no longer have a role to play in the mimetism game: I reject the other. I do not listen anymore to the advice of a colleague who is seeking the same position as I am; I become nervous when I see a man looking at my wife with insistance, and I may remember nothing from a meeting I attended because I envy the person who is conducting the meeting.

Still, if we are not careful enough, the model can easily turn into a rival or, at least, be perceived as such. The most common case is that of the mimetic desire for a promotion, a recognition, an object, or a person each of whom claims the exclusive ownership and feels dispossessed by the other. You taught me how to use such a computer program. Well now, I consider myself better than you and therefore should get the promotion.

The slightest grain of dust, whether real or imaginary, can block the harmonious gearing of our three brains. Jealousy sets in, along with acrimony. The relationship in a couple, or in a group, is tense. Moreover, contact between individuals could lead to an escalation of mimetic rivalry corroborated by the first brain (which provides intellectual justifications) and by the second brain (which engages in emotions). Then, empathy turns into dissension, and positive mimicry as a source of learning is unfortunately jammed.

The escalation of this dynamic sometimes prompts me to perceive the other not only as a rival but also as an obstacle, which can, unfortunately, become an obsession. This situation will create and nourish a certain aggressiveness whose origin is sometimes forgotten but which can last and become unbearable for me and for the people next to me. My clinical experience allows me to confirm that this is also the origin of a large number of psychological and social pathologies.

The model and the rival are fortunately not set in stone. Therefore, depending on the circumstances, our attitude can change from one pole to the other, vis-à-vis the same person. It is a universal attitude that I gladly illustrate by giving the example of a playground where we see Peter "hating" Paul when the latter wants to snatch the ball from his hands. By contrast, we can also see how that same Peter admires Paul when climbing a wall and trying to imitate him to learn the art of climbing.

Nowadays, thanks to much research dedicated to mirror neurons and carried out in the most prestigious international laboratories, we know that the mimetic mechanisms initiate the actions of the other two brains and not the reverse. Our operating system is therefore pre-rational, the logical, ethical, and moral justifications come at a second stage - to reinforce these mechanisms, or to block them. Then, it is our mimetic brain, the third brain, which directly places us into the hominization (or "human") state through our relationship with others.

Understanding well the mechanisms of this movement is the only way to subdue it, or at least master it better to avoid useless and futile rivalries which could become a constant part of our daily life. This has led to building a new metapsychology or introducing a new dynamic that helped me cure many pathologies during my clinical practice. It became possible to a consider new anthropology that, without transferring me into an irenic (or "peaceful") world, allows me to imagine a new social and viable model for human beings.

CHAPTER 2

FROM PSYCHIATRIC HOSPITAL TO LEARNING FACTORY

Fifty-plus years of activity in a psychiatric hospital allowed me to understand and elaborate a fundamental definition of what a disabled person is about: it is someone who cannot be alone. Neither to move, nor to eat, nor to work, nor to live.

Sciatica or flu cripples us. Healing isn't just about having no symptoms or suffering. It is effective when we come out of isolation to reintegrate into the social and work environment. It is then that we spontaneously say to ourselves: "I am finally cured".

The individual with a mental disability is often punished twice: on the one hand, he cannot be alone, therefore autonomous; however, he has, in addition, some difficulties in integrating into the social world to establish a positive and mutually fruitful relationship with the other. This relationship is necessarily mimetic and constitutive of the human being. On the other hand, he is in isolation; therefore, unable to build himself and even more deeply immersed in his disability. As Carl Gustav Jung and Victor Frankl once said: "To live, a man needs to give meaning to his life. Therefore, if he is imprisoned, in his isolation he loses the meaning of life. He simply gives up on life itself".

I have worked on the painful issue of isolation in all the psychiatric hospitals where I have practiced. I have seen patients who were well taken care of in terms of chemical treatments. However, they were terribly alone because of the nature and the severity of the illness and the intensity of the treatments, which have contributed to making them close in on themselves. They were isolated and barely able to speak or interact with each other. I saw them locked up and, above all, abandoned in the absence of a meaningful project capable of mobilizing and motivating them. Thus, they are considered useless because they are different. Here, the meaningful project is the work. And, indeed, the more they are separated from interdividuality, the less they are able to practice an activity or a work.

We have, in spite of ourselves, accepted a lot of conventional ideas that we no longer even try to question. One of them, which prevails in our Western societies, is based on the principle that one must first learn, then train himself before being able to work. To be able to grasp the theory intellectually before putting it into practice. I believe this is an absurd idea, one based on the incongruous belief that "real knowledge" is acquired in books and only books.

I have studied for many years in books. This was the prerequisite step for passing exams and becoming a doctor. However, it was not in the solitude of my room but next to my masters that I really learned the know-how and skills of my profession.

I remember this little story about a patient whom I had examined during my internship. Confident in my intellectual knowledge, I had tested his patellar reflex in vain. Despite the little taps I gave on his kneecap, scrupulously following the "instructions" learned in my books, his leg remained immobile. Facing this abnormal situation, I was distraught, fearing a neurological problem. I called my master to inquire about the case at hand. Imperturbable, he visited the patient, asking him to strongly and tightly squeeze his hands against each other. Focusing on his hands, the patient reacted immediately to the patellar test. No book had taught me to divert the patient's attention so that the reflex could unfold beyond the patient's control.

I experienced the same problem when I started to learn how to use a computer. I read a lot of manuals, in vain. If I handle my tablet and my smartphone properly today, it is because someone was kind enough to sit next to me and teach me the required gestures and patiently show me the way. Then all I had to do was simply imitate him or her.

I remain, since my studies, an apostle of the initiatory approach, based on the transmission of knowledge between the master and the student, between the model and the disciple. The initiatory approach implies interdividuality, and through it, desire and imitation - one cannot initiate oneself.

This approach does not exclude but, on the contrary, integrates. The one whose model remains, in my eyes, the builder of cathedrals who first learned to polish the stone under the guidance of the master. Then, if they have the desire and the capabilities, they become sculptors, then masters and initiators. We learn by doing, and we work by learning...

Le Mans, January 2018. I spent my first day at the AMIPI learning factory. I came to assess in the field the possibility of extending the limits of my theory concerning social interpretation through imitation. This factory is a UPAI (manufacturing, learning and integration factory) and like any factory, it is subject to production deadlines, yield, quality, cost-efficiency, and reactivity. We can see tables that display, for each sector, the number of parts produced or to be produced, daily, weekly, or monthly. Here, the products are sophisticated: they are electrical harnesses meant to be used in the automobile industry, equipping high-end cars.

Now, Antoine is sitting at his production table, concentrating on the cables he will be installing in a certain order. He jumps when I call him out. He hadn't seen me coming. He takes a deep breath before raising his head and smiling at me. I can imagine the effort he has to make. His workstation is essential to the whole chain. In case he is absent, it is imperative that someone replace him in order not to jeopardize the entire production system.

At first, he seems shy, but then he relaxes. He talks about his days: waking up at 6 a.m., cycling by bike for over two kilometers to reach the middle of the countryside, patiently ignoring the bad weather. Remembering the timetables, it is quite essential for him to catch the bus which will leave him near the factory. Since the death of his parents, he is staying at his sister's home in company with his nephews who are not always easy to handle. He likes the job. "I am bored at home" he says. The television news he follows diligently. The high dosage of Xanax pills he takes every morning - "it relaxes me," he mentions. Antoine can neither read nor write and his drawings are those of a 2-year-old child. But here, he is not asked to read, write, or draw. He is just required to work with his hands. And he is quite capable of doing so.

Antoine keeps in mind, more or less, the difficult times he suffered through before finding himself behind his production table. Maryse Vendre remembers very well the teenager she met for the first time in 1976. He was diagnosed with autism. He was flattened, did not speak, and did not move except in his moments of crisis. Against all odds, she succeeded in making him work. Work that heals. For months, some operators showed him a simple but useful gesture that he needed to remember and repeat. The team leader explained to him his interest in making it. For months, he did not react. Then, one day, something happened suddenly. He started to work. It took him long years to move forward and to progress.

Antoine was a bet for Maryse Vendre – one of many who work or have worked here. The gestures he uses have become more complex as he evolved. Alone with his illness, he would have been a drag on himself and his family, or a human vegetable, abandoned in some hospice. Unhappy and useless. At the factory, Antoine has become an operator almost like the others. A little more anxious, more reluctant to change, a little less versatile, but just as useful to the production chain.

This essential knowledge composed of utilitarian gestures beneficial to the economy, the company, and the society, created a major therapeutic transformation. Antoine entered the virtuous circle of interdividuality when he understood its interest. He imitated when he realized that an entire factory was depending on the gestures they taught him. He is now a hard worker, but he has a small problem: his age. Antoine is sixty years old. The age when most people (and the companies they work for) start thinking of retirement. And he is terribly afraid of getting "bored" in his next life...

I have cited Antoine's case, but I could just as well have talked about Pierre, Ernest, or any of the 150 operators who run the Le Mans factory, or the 700 other operators of the AMIPI learning factories that I have visited. These operators have a peculiarity: they all suffer from a mental disability. However, according to their six supervisors, they are not "disabled": just simple operators bound by industrial constraints. In addition, not a single one of these supervisors occupies an educational function (a function which does not exist here, deliberately): they are engineers, managers, HRDs and, behind the workstations, they only see employees, more or less fast learners or executors, more or less versatile, more or less happy or anxious or stressed. Like any other employees in any business.

At the factory, Antoine and the others didn't just learn how to properly perform their tasks. They have learned alterity: a fundamental lesson about how to exchange with the other with an interdividuality approach. First with their master - who initiated them, taking them out of isolation and consequently beyond their disability with the gesture they had to imitate in order to reproduce it at will and appropriate it. Then with their chiefs to whom they must report. Finally, with their colleagues. A worker, even an autonomous one, is an integral part of a production chain. Here, it is composed of 18 operators. Each worker in this chain patiently waits to receive prepped material to progress through the workflow. Everyone knows he is important to the chain since his work is influencing the work of others, upstream and downstream. What is more rewarding than knowing yourself essential?

They have also learned how to discover meaning-- first in their work and then, by extension, in their other activities. This apprenticeship occurs because the chain linking them has a dual purpose: direction and significance. Direction, because the production line cannot operate hazardously; it has to follow a sequential and strict order. Because this chain is not established haphazardly; it has a goal, an aim, and of course there are some expected outcomes. Herein lies the big difference between the factory and the ergo therapy. At the first, the production is useful and the operator knows he is indispensable. Trying to overcome his handicap is for him an effort full of meaning. Drawing or playing with modeling clay is, for example, necessary at some point in the therapy process. However, this activity should be limited in time, otherwise, the individual will literally walk around in circles, with no outcomes. Yes, it is sometimes an important step; however, it is not enough to give meaning to the work and therefore to the individual's life.

I had already sensed this meaning while working with Pascal Duquenne, the legendary hero of "The Eighth Day," a movie which had received many awards when it was released in 1996, including for best actor at the Cannes Festival. Pascal is a great actor. And he also suffers from Trisomy 21 (sometimes referred to as "Down's Syndrome"). He started his career with this film where, despite his disability, he played a big role. He "came out" of his disabled status thanks to another great actor, Daniel Auteuil, who served as his model, by giving meaning to his life and valuing his work. The release of the film reflected it. Pascal Duquenne then outdid himself. Since then, he has had a great career.

In reality, disability is only a part of a much larger problem that affects our entire 21st-century society. A society where non-work is considered a Holy Grail and universal income as a given in the coming years when robots will replace humans in production. A society where the organization is seen only as a place where people and robots produce with one unique aim: to generate profits.

This perspective terrifies me. I fully agree with Cédric Villani, who, when asked by the President of the French Republic to work on artificial intelligence, said that we need to work to fulfill ourselves. Because it makes us feel useful to ourselves and society. Unemployment is not only causing damage to our health because of a lack of sustainable income but also because of the loss of self-esteem and dignity.

Such a society seems to ignore an essential principle: a company is foremost a place where men and women develop themselves, where personality and individuality are forged, and where an individual can be recognized and elevated because of his contribution to humanity. This, and I weigh my words, cannot be built outside of an activity, which is part of a collective process, a theater of interdividuality. Its dimension is not only financial. It is also sociological. More specifically, it is to adults what school is to children: a place where learning can help improve on the professional side but also where social and societal aspects should prevail. A child needs other children to build himself and become autonomous. An adult needs other adults to continue his work which extends throughout a lifetime.

We already know that in the next fifteen years, 50% of current jobs will no longer exist: drivers, blue-collar workers, many white-collar workers, waiters, surgeons, radiologists, back and middle offices in banks, perhaps also writers and journalists, among others, will be replaced by robots.

Already, we see robots reigning and intervening in Amazon's giant warehouses- several tens of thousands of square meters where the only humans are at the end of the chain, to deposit packages in delivery trucks, a task that also will soon be executed by robots. More jobs will be created, I'm sure. But, if we are not careful enough, someone will probably reserve them for creative people, for people with very high potential; in short, for an elite who will be surrounded by armies of unemployed.

I heard that less time allocated to work will allow more time for leisure. This, too, is an elitist speech that scandalizes me. Needless to say, it does not address the overwhelming majority of the population. People will become flabby in front of their television. This life will isolate them more and more. And, more dangerously, trap them in their neuroses and psychoses, destroy them and prevent them from living with dignity. In other respects, from an economic point of view, at a time when States are impoverished, what kind of universal income can claim to be the equivalent of a salary, meeting basic needs and perhaps some leisure?

At the AMIPI factories, I met some operators who delightedly told me of the independence gained thanks to their salary, the apartment they can finally rent, the gifts they can offer to their loved ones (the pleasure of giving that surpasses that of receiving!), the last restaurant they went to with their spouse. The opportunity of reaching the level of materialistic self-sufficiency.

But beyond the salary (superior to disabled adult allowances) they told me about their happiness at work, especially those who had been excluded from normal life for a long period of time because of their disability. They finally felt useful: in a nutshell, just existing as human beings.

Because work, as we will see in the following pages, is not an activity that only allows you to earn a living. It is much more than that. It is the best opportunity to build oneself by developing multidimensional, cognitive, and affective capabilities, and above all relationship abilities; that is to say, mimetic.

Let us never forget that it is in the relationship where the self is built and where humankind progresses. We are steeped in alterity since Adam, created by God from clay according to the Bible, but above all in the image of His desire, which is the desire to create. God has placed in humankind an exceptional capacity for creation and recreation. Man is the only animal in charge of re-creating itself until its death, in a process of transformation through relationship with the other, and therefore by initiation. This initiation is an agony, a ritual of death and resurrection. To tell the truth, it is a daily evolution, leaving yesterday to die in order to create today and tomorrow.

When the human being no longer has the possibility of re-creating himself, his environment, and his destiny, when he creates nothing, he is actually nothing. At that moment, he vanishes.

In this perspective, a company manufactures objects, but it also builds humans. Work is a guarantee of humanity sustainability. We must therefore sustain it, for itself, for us, to continue the task of the cathedrals' builders who molded their personality as they transformed and sculpted the stone. Whereas the stone freed itself from the weight of the substance which surrounded it, the craftsman realized then that he also had been profoundly molded. In fact, he had molded himself. They then passed on the knowledge to the next generation. Like any worker or factory operator who develops himself by manufacturing, then transmits to the other who, in turn, improves himself further by manufacturing.

What about tomorrow? This is the big question. We must start to design the work of the future, the factory of tomorrow that cannot be replaced by artificial intelligence. We must immediately mobilize ourselves to preserve humankind vis a vis robots and artificial intelligence. We must, in other words, continue to manufacture Homo Anthropos rather than thinking of Homo Deus. The adjustment of the future society will not happen without you and me, without each individual who constitutes the society itself.

Otherwise, humanity will disappear with the reign of robots; it will no longer have any meaning or "raison d'être".

CHAPTER 3

WHAT IS INTELLIGENCE?

Jeanne is forty-three years old. A brilliant operator, her versatility is quite valuable to the factory. She is familiar with the complex mechanism of manufacturing wires and knows how to cut, press, and assemble. She also has learned how to properly use the tools and how machines function - a skill of which I personally remain ignorant.

She was promoted because of her meticulousness. Actually, she is a quality controller. Therefore, she can, at a glance, detect the smallest defects, and alert the operator in charge and, when needed, the team leader. At the AMIPI factory in Nantes (where she has worked since she was eighteen) and as in any other factory in the group, customers are high-end car manufacturers. They are very demanding on quality. Thus, the product cannot be defective in any way.

Jeanne is self-confident. Still, she hasn't always been. In sixth grade, her teachers and her family had given up on her. She was regarded as too "dumb;" she hadn't learned to read and write. She often "freaked out," as she said with a small smile, on the smallest occasion. Considered intellectually disabled, she could not even find a single support to accept her. She was moving in a vicious circle -- an idle person with no sense of hope or goal in life, sinking deeper and deeper into her isolation, because of her disability which didn't really have a name. Experts had qualified her as stupid and slow. She was self-destructive because she had no opportunity to build herself.

The factory was first viewed by those around her as an opportunity to get her out of her loneliness and make her useful and productive through work. In reality, no one believed she could engage in a regular working life with its constraints and pressure. This view had not taken into account the value of working in a team. Jeanne quickly understood that she was engaging in a collective endeavor and that she was part of something greater than herself as an individual. This new purpose was enough to make her feel more responsible. Someone believed that she had potential since she had been entrusted with a real task on which the tasks of other operators in the chain depended. Therefore, despite her limitations, she strived to do her best.

However, for the first few days, she was afraid to work. She didn't even dare to say "I don't know" or "I made a mistake". She became anxious because she was expecting to hear the answers she had always heard since early childhood: "Idiot, moron, too stupid, everyone gets there, but you are still incapable of progress..." But she was pleasantly surprised to hear, instead: "You are capable, I will show you how to do it".

Here, they trusted her, and she learned to believe in herself. She discovered unique capabilities. In particular, an amazing visual memory. This aptitude evolved little by little because of the demands of her manual tasks and the working environment in which she progressed and in which she was an essential cog.

Still, she can't read. Instead, she now knows how to take a mental picture of the information she needs to keep in mind n order to fulfill her tasks. For example, the "default code" of a cable cut, which she puts in the right column, in the inspection books; therefore, she can accumulate bits of information and store them up her memory. This reassuring memory has also transformed her personal life, through tiny details such as recognizing the name of a street or remembering the location of a bus station she has previously "photographed" with her eyes, or a price in a supermarket, or the recipient of a letter.

For years, Jeanne had lived as a mentally disabled person. She had been considered as such because of her inability to concentrate and, by implication, to master mental acuity, such as the ability to read or to solve easy mathematic problems. Her intelligence had been smothered. Because even if she is not gifted in intellectual studies, Jeanne is very intelligent. She is a genius in dexterity, with her manual skills. And by her incredible way of instinctively focusing on her work -- for hours, if necessary. Many others wouldn't resist.

Jeanne had been systematically criticized since childhood for being mentally slow. At the factory, tests had shown that she was no slower than average, especially in manual work. Her learning pace took a little longer, which needed more patience. But upon arrival, she seems to be fast. I still don't really have an explanation for that. Was her slowness entirely innate, or was it the result of some conditioning factors, or simply due to her reactions to continually being reproached for being "slow"?

Then there's Olivier, whose sadistic teacher struck his fingers with an iron ruler. The question remains: is Olivier lacking intelligence, or is he simply the victim of a trauma that has never been recognized and from which he has not yet been able to overcome? At the factory, he is a production line assistant and manages a chain of forty people. He is forty-seven years old, with two children, and three grandchildren. But when he speaks of this school teacher, he is still afraid and he trembles. At six years old, he was so afraid of making a mistake that he stopped studying. He said one day: "Reading reminds me of M. Rostan, and it's hard". Olivier, who was considered unintelligent, left school at twelve without having really learned anything. Still, as soon as he opens a book, the image of his teacher, the so-called torturer, comes back to his mind and reminds him of his painful past. However, at the factory, his work is excellent, and he has received successive promotions thanks to his manual abilities and perseverance. Olivier was a martyred child with a disability. Still, he is not disabled; he is quite intelligent.

The work at the factory offered to Olivier the opportunity to develop himself. He plays different roles at the same time. He is an operator, a line assistant, a father, and a grandfather. However, he remains a human being first with dignity. Remaining unemployed would have condemned him to be even more buried in his neurosis and inability to live a normal life, plagued by anxiety and nightmares, subject to depression and exclusion. He would have been annihilated. But his trauma is not exceptional.

During my stays in the United States, I had the opportunity to visit hospitals reserved for war veterans (operated by the US Veterans Administration). The veterans' post-traumatic stress syndromes have incapacitated them and created very long-term blockage. Tired out and stupefied by various tranquilizers, they have ceased thinking properly and using their intellect. But they are still intelligent. In fact, what they need is the opportunity to rediscover and rebuild everything that remains deep down inside them.

I taught humanities for a long period at the Sorbonne in Paris. I have supervised doctoral theses and I have seen brilliant generations of students passing by, able to discourse for hours on Freud or on Plato. But, most aberrantly, they were completely helpless in front of a machine, would it be a photocopier, a scanner, or sometimes a computer. They were always desperately asking for help. Simply put, they had no manual intelligence. This is, to my knowledge, also disability. Still, we will not designate them as disabled people. They had another form of intelligence, called intellectual. They were, like Jeanne, like most of us, capable of achieving certain things, but unable to properly accomplish others. Or at least for a certain time.

I don't know anyone who has developed all the forms of intelligence that are specific to a human being such as the intelligence of mathematics, letters, music, precise manual work, space, abstraction, logic, emotions... Fortunately! But on the other hand, we would be helpless if we all had only one form of intelligence to the detriment of all the others. What would happen If we were a society composed of geniuses in mathematics, but incapable of writing a poem or building a house? A society only develops if its members are collectively intelligent. And to become intelligent, there is, to my knowledge, a golden recipe, insufficiently exploited: work.

I don't know anyone, either, who doesn't wear in him any of these forms of intelligence. The real challenge, which will arise more and more in our society, consists in knowing how to detect and nourish in each person the capabilities he or she possesses, which are useful to the community. And then take the necessary time, depending on each individual pace, to help him/her develop the unique ability that characterizes him/her and makes him/her valuable to the group. We certainly will not deny the difficulties that some may encounter during this challenging journey. In addition, we will make no one believe that there are no obstacles in the attempt to learn, progress, and improve.

By claiming that everything is easy and immediately workable, we will definitely contribute to letting the individual sink deeper into his disability as was the case for Jeanne during her childhood. Obsessed with what they lack and what we consider "unspeakable", they forget to see what they have to offer. We evolve by knowing and learning to deal with our weaknesses. Therefore, we need help to overcome them and smartly circumvent them.

Our society is sick by dint of over-treatment and multiple remedies. There is a serious risk of abuse and exaggeration.

Society becomes sick when we ourselves become the disability, with weaknesses and blockages, and when we cease to think and act like humans, with infinite strengths and abilities. A human may have a disability, but he or she is a human foremost.

Unlike what is happening in psychiatric hospitals, I did not see comfort or pity in the learning factories where I immersed myself. More importantly, I witnessed the professionalism of a structured work environment which was, to me, more reassuring and promising than everything else. Overprotection has never been an ideal way to progress.

Here, at AMIPI, we don't lie and we don't unconditionally try to please. We consider that a disabled person is not a kindergarten child that we just applaud when wearing a pasta necklace for Mother's Day! Errors are pointed out without ever stigmatizing the worker. The worker is again accompanied, and confidence is renewed. Moreover, Issues are identified, and the way of solving them is recalled to move forward and progress. Without a doubt, the need to follow strict rules and regulations and adopt quality production standards in these learning factories requires all workers to outdo themselves. Producing quality goods makes everyone very proud, as Sami told me one day. He was helping his brother-in-law repair his car when he discovered under the hood an electrical harness from the AMIPI factories. Looking for the label to discern the name of the one who made it (this is a requirement in these factories), he sees his own name stamped on it. From that moment, Sami discovered he is different. Multi-talented...

We all have intelligence and aptitudes, and we all claim the right to work. Working allows you to exist. To be "somebody". To develop intelligence and skills. Work keeps you standing upright, supports you, keeps you going, and preserves your dignity. Working makes you human.

CHAPTER 4

FROM HAND TO SYNAPSES

After the fall of the Romanian dictator Nicolae Ceausescu in 1989, the world discovered, horrified, the big disaster of orphanages in Romania where tens of thousands of children were locked up like wild beasts, deprived of affection, clean food, human relationship, action, game, with no basic mental and physical care. Several NGOs then mobilized, intending to help, bringing these children the benefit of medical examinations and appropriate treatments giving scientists the opportunity to carry out many medical studies.

Among these studies, those of Serban Ionescu and Daniel Stern deserve our attention. Both start from the same observation: MRI imaging revealed that these children had atrophied brains, as if they had shrunk over the years. When placed in a normal and affectionate environment, these children had at their disposal, among other things, some games and more importantly interactions with other human beings. Thereafter, MRIs carried out at regular intervals revealed amazing brain developments. More specifically, these developments occurred principally because of the resilient capacity of neurons and their synapses to regenerate and multiply as affectionate and respectful interactions and emotional blossoming took place, thus generating learning and behavioral progression.

The human brain is of such exceptional plasticity that scientists have not finished exploring it. My friend, the neuropsychiatrist Boris Cyrulnik, dedicated a great amount of study to the plasticity of the brain. He claims that the damage caused to the brain is not irreversible, as long as it continues to be emotionally and intellectually stimulated.

It is commonly said that the brain "muscles itself". We know that memory can be trained and thus become more efficient with time. In each of us, specific areas of the cortex develop themselves and are enriched with new synapses. This means increased connections between neurons as we solicit and mobilize them to carry out our activities. For example, areas dedicated to smell and taste are more developed among oenologists. Those related to skillful manual work are more present among craftsmen than among clerks. We can see them "in movement" on PET scans, reflecting the activity of neurons, following a given action.

I saw, on these screens, the brain of a pianist listening to a sonata by Beethoven. It was enlightened with a thousand fires, while for a non-pianist, infinitely fewer neural circuits were formed. The same goes for a football player who is viewing a match. The movements he sees already developed the circuits. The mimicry does the rest. As a matter of fact, on the control screens, his brain lights up with an explosion of a variety of colors. However, it appears much less in the case of non-football fans, where circuits are not as pronounced because they are not stimulated.

I could add more examples. At the AMIPI factory in Nantes, when Jeanne discovered the strength of her visual memory (that she considered as the pillar of her intelligence) she put her brain to work doing real mental gymnastics. If they had been carried out, the medical imaging, which is more and more precise, would have revealed a physical development of neurons in the areas of the cortex where memories are stored (the parietal, temporal, and occipital lobes).

Similarly, at the AMIPI plant in Le Mans, Antoine gradually exited the prostration into which his autism has plunged him, left him to vegetate in his corner. Simple gestures with a useful purpose that he carried out every day at the factory have contributed to awakening neurons in the brain areas affected by the movement. Neural circuits are created with each new gesture learned. Antoine's brain has gradually regenerated, allowing him to gain the autonomy he shows today, both in his work and in his personal life.

Jeanne, Antoine and the other operators with whom I have regularly spoken have literally strengthened the capabilities of their brains because they were given the opportunity to do it. At the factory, they were trusted. This gave them confidence in themselves and in their ability to keep advancing. They were finally comfortable in their new life, happy, and endowed with the desire to improve their learning and enhance their talents, by being imbued with the same desire that they saw around them. They imitated, and they worked hard. This has driven them into a virtuous circle. In fact, work has brought them pride in producing something valuable. It has allowed them to rebuild themselves. To become somebody. Their neurons were being challenged, and they were developing. This will continue as long as their hands are regularly sending messages to these neurons in order to stimulate them and receive, in return, the nerve impulse that instigates and guides their movements.

The practice of psychiatry led me to reject the idea of Descartes when asserting the duality of the human being, pretending that there is a total separation of body and spirit. The soul, disembodied and superior to substance, has, according to Descartes, nothing to do with the body itself. But I saw that a pill or an injection could calm the psychic and spiritual anxieties of my patients. However, a medicine does not cure the causes of depression or annihilate the reasons behind extreme agitation. It can calm the mind and thus opens a dialogue with the patient, when necessary, to find a way out of the crisis. Knowing that a medicine affects the brain in order to influence the mood, another path comes to light for serious consideration: the mood influences the brain.

When Diane arrived at the Le Mans factory, she was coming out of six years of inactivity, boredom, and apathy life at home. Her only occupation was taking care of her domestic rabbit. Her parents worked; her brother followed a normal schooling trajectory. Staying at home, she waited for one day to pass and the next one to begin. Days that were identical and, unfortunately, unproductive. "My childhood was difficult in terms of friendship," Diane says modestly. She described how she was shoved aside, and suffered from her loneliness: too slow, too disruptive, too emotional. Still, at twenty-six, her relatives keep saying to her that she behaves like a twelve-year-old girl. "Years ago, a psychologist had confirmed the fatal verdict: He told me that I was slow, that I hardly can perform two actions at the same time and I suffer from a lack of maturity". Diane was disappointed, with no real hope of moving forward in her life. She took this diagnosis for granted. It is quite possible that she molded herself into this frame, which unfortunately had become a role model for her.

However, at the factory, Diane accomplishes things that a child could not do. She now works in the "store," upstream of the chain of production. She is in charge of preparing the kits intended for each team, sorting big quantities of wires, each with a specific terminal, and preparing packages with references composed of five digits, using the precise counting scale. Diane is certainly slower than average, but also more scrupulous than average. The kits she puts together are impeccable. She never makes a mistake; there is never an oversight.

At the factory, she gained in speed and above all in maturity. Neural circuits were formed from the beginning of her work as an operator, thanks to the meticulous and consistent work executed by her hands. She advanced through successive learning stages. Each learning, induced under the effect of mimicry, has created products and, at the same time, developed a bit more of the brain. Her neurons regenerated, then multiplied.

Since then, Diane, whom those around her considered lost, passed her driver's exam and received a license. She plans to become independent and rent a flat. She hopes to integrate herself into a "normal" working environment by finding work in the animal sector. And above all, never stop working. She proudly says: "It makes me feel good. I receive a salary, I develop myself, I improve, and I converse normally with my colleagues. I am no longer the same. It was difficult at the beginning, I didn't think I would get there, I had to learn everything quickly. I finally succeeded. It's strange. At the factory, I grew up..."

Diane grew up when she stopped being overprotected. When she had, instead, to be productive. Her mindset was forced to learn, to control all parts of her body (including, of course, her brain), to "fill her life, then her being". Overprotection, in this sense, is a form of exclusion leading to a state of no activity, with no possibility to improve and progress.

In the past, children who worked incorrectly and poorly, who were dissipated, too slow or too restless, were sometimes scolded, but above all loved. They were not stigmatized because of their diminished appetite for the intellectual side of life. They had the possibility of choosing a convenient path appropriate to their situation. Despite the difficulties, they had to move forward, at least meeting the level of trust placed in them. They were empowered, and even if they did not all show the same level of maturity, they developed and achieved against all odds. Great progress !

It is this same technique that is actually implemented in the learning factories. I met some operators who have been surprised by their own capabilities and know-how when at a time, elsewhere, they had been regarded as "handicapped".

Most of them claim loudly "I can accomplish this activity!". They are now enthusiastic about taking part in a new learning process and discovering that this set of know-hows can be transferred to their private life. For example, they now have the confidence to fill in a health care reimbursement sheet without hesitation or hiding behind an "I don't know," because at the factory they fill out documents that are well more complex.

It is known that the hands, through valuable manual work, contribute to the development of synapses. However, it is also known that this is not enough. There is a need to create an appropriate work environment that will contribute to building up the "being". In addition, respect and trust are essential characteristics to immerse in the learning process and nourish the relationship as well as discipline and rigor. All these requirements serve to make the individual more responsible. As a matter of fact, in these learning factories, cuddling and pampering are not allowed.

One supervisor told me one day: "We don't handle kid gloves when we interact with workers". We sometimes are very demanding and tough. Therefore, we are not permissive and we don't consider that a disability should favor forbearance. We know that by being always lenient we would not only fail in solving the issue but also, we will perpetuate the problem, and allow the individual to dive more and more into his disability He added: "as in any business, we remain open to discussion when facing a problem. We reassure and strive to reduce the stress level. However, we always remind the operator that there is an obligation to fulfill his or her duties. Isn't that also the case in traditional companies?".

Having a goal to achieve (in factories, the number of items to be manufactured) is, in itself, a challenge that pushes people to break records. I might be sad and anxious. Still, the rest of the people within the chain are depending on me. Workers in these factories learn to put their problems aside and move. One small step after the other leads to the future. Is it too complicated? I would say it is more simply human. But, in our society, humanity tends to vanish.

I saw operators who had been excluded from school because of their inability to concentrate and their great agitation. I had a friend, Jean-Pierre, who was very restless at school. We would call him today hyperactive, and we would give him medication. Our teacher had found another method: he asked him to stand on a table, carrying a small piece of furniture, trying not to fall off the table. After a few minutes, he calmed down. Jean-Pierre pursued his education until the baccalaureate, always more active than the others, but having gradually learned to stay more or less quiet.

Restless? Unable to concentrate? In the factories, the operators are sitting in front of their respective work stations, focusing on the job, meticulously executing it with their hands with the precision of a goldsmith. Attentive to what they can perform, their so-called lack of attention disappears as if by magic. Their brains have learned to calm down. Someone and something have finally channeled their energy. They are relieved and valued...

CHAPTER 5

THE MODEL, DRIVING FORCE

We are not free to not imitate. Mimicry, as we have seen, is related to our physical, neurological, and psychic states. Fortunately, it is the engine that makes us learn, progress, and advance. More importantly, become a living human being.

I learned much more standing beside a master I saw examining a patient than in books. I learned by carefully listening to him but, more again, through the way he examines patients with a stethoscope, listening to their heart, lungs and their organs; how he listens to them, and thoroughly examines them. I saw him sometimes heartily taking their hand to reassure them and reduce their distress. Therefore, I have been formed also by imitating my masters. They were my models.

If Antoine, Olivier, Jeanne, Diane, and the others had been placed into their work environment without human support and without the confidence and trust which have elevated them as a springboard, they would have immediately been banned, excluded again, and ruthlessly imprisoned once more in their disability: condemned.

The intelligence of learning factories is to fully adhere to and apply the medieval model of compagnonnage (mentorship). This model is mainly based on the connection that is transmitted from the master to the pupil. Then, this connection is strengthened with patience and trust, through the challenging journey of two persons, each progressing at his own pace thanks to accompaniment and orientation. Therefore, there is a need to fully adhere to the model and refine it through a hierarchy of role models. However, all concerned people should be aware of their respective role models and critical responsibility.

The first model, the closest one, including geographically, is the "elders". Someone who is part of a group of experienced operators who suffer also from a disability. They informally coach and guide the new entrant through his path. This is what I would call horizontal mimetism. These elders followed the same process of learning and went through the same difficulties. They are not superior; they are equals. They know a little more because they have already learned and overcome the obstacles. Their enthusiasm and willingness to work, to share, and to produce are immediately sensed by the mirror neurons of the newcomer. Will my colleague be able to catch the wire? He aroused my desire. My mirror neurons activate and the need to imitate is strongly making itself felt. Moreover, the need to imitate is felt well since the colleagues perform according to the horizontal model.

My friend Andrew Meltzoff, head of the Institute for Learning and Brain Sciences at the University of Washington, conducted an experiment proving the existence of the mimicry of the intention, therefore of the desire. In the presence of a group composed of very young children. He grabbed a pen and tried to uncap it, but he failed. Identical pens were given to the children. They actually succeeded in removing the cap. They had not only imitated his gesture; they had understood his need and intention, therefore his desire, although he failed to uncap the pen. By imitation, the desire to uncap the pen, the intention, and the action had become theirs, they went beyond the incomplete action of their model, and they accomplished it.

And then there is vertical mimicry where we can look at the example of the leader, who becomes a reference, a mimetic model who must know his role as a model and as a teacher and accordingly assume his responsibility.

The first degree of the vertical model is a bet for AMIPI... and it is a success. The actors here are "training assistant". Odile is one of them. Considered "lost" according to the traditional education system and by her family, she entered the factory in 1988. No one around her really believed she would stay there. She was perceived as too slow, too restless, and too messy. In conclusion, too disabled. But, at her workstation, Odile proved to be one of the best. Other operators recognized her skills and informally ask for her help when needed. After a few years, her status as training assistant become official.

Still, Odile can't read or write. However, she is in charge of training the newly hired workers, as well as the temporary ones who do not have a disabled status and who are called in as reinforcement to back up the production team during peak periods or to replace those absent during holidays. She was moved the first time she had to deal with the trainees. Terribly shy, she stuttered. Then her trainee students complimented her. They were happy with what they had achieved and she was reassured and quietened. Living with her parents, Odile smiles when she talks about her job and usually says: "At least, I'm useful for something."

Odile is an excellent role model. She doesn't judge or comfort. She lets the operators (and trainees) assume their responsibilities, treats them as adults and does not let them complain about their illness. "If they cry, I leave them to cry, I come back afterward." Odile has enough confidence in herself and is so sure of her abilities at work that she is not afraid of the rivalry of those she has already formed and trained. These trainees know fully that she is there to tutor and help not to judge. They also know that they just have to imitate her gestures to learn and improve. By being present at work and interacting, both parties feel alive and useful to each other. Confined at home, doing nothing, they would have died. It's the main difference between life and death, between being and non-being, and between having and being.

The second level of the vertical model includes the production line assistant who supervises a group of operators. It is a "proximity manager" who can intervene quickly. He is always present on-site within his team, to help when a problem occurs. His function is primarily utilitarian. Considered knowledgeable, he is recognized by his peers for his vast knowledge and subsequent experience. In whatever way or manner, his status and authority prevent rivalries from arising and disputes from happening. He can do what others can't. That's all.

In the beginning, when Olivier was promoted, there was jealousy. Others were looking at him with envious eyes. However, this attitude changed and the envious feeling disappeared quickly when he proved to be up to the challenges of the job requirements. He helped the operators, responded to their various inquiries, answered their questions, and supported them fully. They finally admitted that he lives up to his responsibility and consequently he became the model to follow. At a given point in time, they were not yet capable of such versatility. Their third brain (mirror neurons), activated by the first brain (reason), did not wake up to claim: "me too".

I experienced the same situation during my medical studies, when, as an intern in hospitals, I and my colleagues criticized the "chief", our mentor, until the day we faced a serious problem with a patient. The "chief" immediately changed the treatment and the next day the patient was feeling better. We then all realized that we were not capable to take his place. We were not ready yet because of our lack of experience and leadership and because we still had many things to learn. Respect for his skills and knowledge stifled all the jealousies and the rivalries.

In the AMIPI factories, as I have already pointed out, the supervisors, those we usually call executives and senior executives elsewhere, are called "chiefs" and they are few in number. It's a deliberate choice, intended to empower operators and line assistants and it is the best way to get everyone to surpass themselves on the path to progress. Therefore, before calling on the "big boss", they try to deal with the problem at hand and develop a certain autonomy in the decision-making process. Then, if problems are not fixed, the "big boss" intervenes.

These supervisors are positioned in the upper levels of the vertical models. They hold the authority and possess the power. The hierarchy is clearly defined, and even if this notion seems obsolete in certain cases and outdated to certain business people, and despite the appearance of start-ups advocating for the horizontal model, my experience has shown me it guarantees the sustainability of the management systems, remains a factor of peace, and ensures good relations between employees.

On one hand, it creates a structure and imposes some benchmarks, a kind of compass that is clearly visible and well known by all. On another hand, whatever one thinks or believes, an employee needs some orientation; more specifically, he needs to know what to do, and whom to refer in case of a problem. An employee looks after a "big model" in which he can recognize himself, that he can follow and on whom to count. A person who, whatever happens, knows more and who can reassure. This is also the reason why, in a company, the boss must always be ahead of those he leads. Otherwise, this boss can no longer serve as a model and a guide. Then, the disorder settles down instead. We have all encountered such situations in our lives.

I believe hierarchy contributes to reducing rivalry. It is a strong remedy. Shakespeare, who was an excellent observer of the human soul and who has studied various pathologies in societies, noted, with great wisdom, that the disappearance of hierarchies in societies and organizations generates rebellion and violence. "*When degree is gone, violence sets in.*" An army is left disordered and divided when, on the field, a soldier ceases to obey the officer in charge, and when the colonel rebels and rises against the general. The rivalry immediately spreads and the battle is then lost.

Today we avoid talking about "hierarchy", and the position of the "boss" is rejected and its role questioned. This is wrong. What we lose in words, we lose it also in values. What we consider unimportant or unnecessary work positions make us doubt our values and mistrust our beliefs. Yet, the most fragile populations still need to structure themselves in order to keep some benchmarks to refer to. From there, they can evolve and progress. In the absence of benchmarks and clear systems, societies will witness a great injustice that affects all populations. This is happening in the health sector, in hospitals. When I was a student, my friends and I used to have "bosses" who were highly regarded as great references in their specialty. Today, hospitals are full of university professors and hospital practitioners. They are excellent health professionals. Still, they lack the aura and the authority. Unfortunately, Models are now disappearing.

At the Le Mans factory, Frédéric is the supervisor. He manages 160 operators, and deals with 3 major customers. His work requires a lot of responsibility and commitment. His physical appearance is imposing and impressive. Therefore reassuring. He knows the job quite well, and he is perfectly aware of all the different functions in the factory. He can rightly claim to be a real model. He is there because he knows the entire business. However, sometimes he does not know enough. Therefore, cannot always provide the right answer or solution and he admits it. In such a case he usually says: "I don't have the answer. Still, I will do my best to have it." Then he takes the time to look for the right answer or solution and makes sure to properly communicate it. That's why he is respected and highly thought of.

For the outside visitor, an important element is immediately striking: the good humor that prevails in the workshops among workers. There are no recriminations or resentments, no complaints or depressions, only a certain determination to collectively reach an understanding where the desire to live together in harmony is put into practice and nourished. The "chief" has a trick that he reveals to me. He uses it to create a mimicry. When he arrives in the morning, even though he is tired, he smiles and gives the impression of being in great shape. The operators unconsciously imitate him modeling their behavior on his. However, when worries appear on his face on certain mornings, he can notice that the operators are more tired than usual. They are less enthusiastic. This is not a weird or inexplicable situation. It is just a physiological matter related to the mirror neurons.

I watched Frederic. He is rigorous, and he imposes a certain discipline and applies systems. He talks about yield (the one who is at the level of the operators) and he speaks about quality, results, and issues. He disregards the handicap because he no longer sees it. He mainly focuses on human being's performances. He is the "elder brother" who sends back a positive image, that of his competencies, achievement, and happiness, and who takes your hand to teach you how to do. He is not a robot. He has empathy and can show some feelings. He is able to say to the others: "Come, we will succeed together." He goes to the front with his troops, using an exceptional interdividual relationship. He is the leader, the indisputable model that many parents have ceased to be.

However, being a leader does not mean annihilating interdividuality, either by amplifying the importance of his role to the detriment of the role of others (not allowing any decision to be taken by others and denying self-actualization) or simply by discouraging them ("you won't make it").

These destructive attitudes depict abusive authority and resentment. They ultimately lead to the same result: to demotivate and eradicate any possibility of progress. These models who do not assume their role and duty cease to become the reference to others and the leader to follow. They simply become counter-models.

Remember, the way we look at the other and the way we treat him are vital to his future.

CHAPTER 6

THE POISON OF RIVALRY

The blueprint of the model is definitely valuable. Still, infinitely fragile. The smallest grain of sand is enough to let the model fall into rivalry. All grains of sand have the same tendency which is to generate rivalry between human beings. In an organization, it could be depicted as follows: I want what the other owns and I do not recognize his right to own it.

A relevant story is taking place every day in the courtyard of a kindergarten. Paul and John are friends until John shows off his red balloon that is apparently much more desirable, in Paul's eyes, than his own green ball. Paul will envy John. He would want to take possession of John's ball at any cost. They will argue, maybe fight, and probably cry.

Later in adult life, a similar scenario shall take place. This time, the object of desire, the source of covetousness, will be a woman (or a man), a promotion at work, a market to conquer, a car, a parking place in the street, etc. The third brain jams the interindividual cursor on the rival's position: "I am able to say or do the same thing, so able to take his place..."

Frédéric, the workshop supervisor, suffered from the rivalry of a newly hired leader line who was nevertheless destined for a successful career in AMPI. But very quickly, the assistant decided to take Frédéric's job and not any other, considering himself more competent. In his mind, he had the right to take Frédéric's job considering the latter as a usurper. Their relationship which was initially cordial (Frédéric was perceived as a model to imitate), has tensed up. The confidence has been lost.

This is a typical example of mimetism perversion which also depicts the case of the line leader who strives to take the place of the model and sets him up as a rival and as an obstacle. The situation became quickly unbearable, leaving a mark and affecting, because of mimetism, the whole factory. AMIPI had to urgently get rid of the line leader.

There are also stingy models. Some are stingy by nature, even selfish with things they do not possess, or with things they possess but can be shared, such as the knowledge and know-how that they are afraid to transmit. These so-called models usually grow by reducing the others. And then there are those who are miserly because they are afraid of being surpassed by their students.

They lack confidence in themselves and act in a way that prevents their students from taking precedence over them, or at least being equal to them. Also, those "so-called models" are extremely anxious and are afraid to be cast into the shadow. Several narcissistic perverts fall into this category. This attitude affects even the relationship between family members. I know parents who are jealous of the success of their children, to the extent that they become exasperated by their success.

These models became rivals because an important element has disappeared from the interdividual relationship. It is simply called: trust. The one that the student puts in the master is paramount otherwise the imitation process would not properly take place. That of the teacher towards the pupil is just as important: it is a clear and strong sign of gratification which shows esteem and respect. But the student is always aware that the master knows more than him Therefore, the master remains a model to imitate. The three brains then work simultaneously. In concert. The first brain (reason) recognizes the superiority of the model because of the knowledge and the trust. The second brain (the emotion) is thankful and grateful. The third brain (the mirror neurons) imitates. This three dimensional brain depict the ideal neural configuration. Still, by ignoring the basic rules of our cerebral functioning, we misunderstand and even jeopardize the whole system. And, sometimes unconsciously, or because of ignorance or simply fear, we put the grain of sand in the mechanism and consequently break the loop.

In a certain number of organizations, rivalry takes place at all levels of the hierarchy. It is sometimes ingrained in the mind of colleagues or developed between departments. It is also nourished by a curious phenomenon that I call the syndrome of "I don't have time". A phenomenon that spreads and grows under the effect of stress and as a result of fierce competition among people, and because of our crazy lifestyle. Concentrated on a recurrent stock or production problem and knocked out by his usual daily life problems, the supervisor keeps repeating to employees for whom he is responsible, the same sentence "I don't have the time". These employees just need help to be able to carry on their work. In such a conflicting situation, the whole group enters a vicious circle: the supervisor does not have time to answer, those who refer to him cannot progress, and eventually, he has even less time to work himself. The outcome is catastrophic. We witness an act of disengagement. The model cuts himself off from his own role of model, of master, and he stops the relationship and the interdividuality. Performance diminishes and the recurrent stock or production problem remains unsolved.

The model is therefore isolated in an ivory tower where he is powerless. Deprived of the leader's authority, employees (but this could also be the case of students in a class) will enter into a dangerous spiral of rivalry. What really matters now is to know which of them will replace him, become the master, and make the decisions. Jealousies and grudges set in. The door opens to endless debate: who should decide? Is it the operator or the line assistant? The regular workflow is then interrupted at all levels of the organization.

The "I don't have time" syndrome appeared in one factory of the AMPI. The general management, which oversees all the factories, was smart enough to put in place new mimetic models to cut short eventual rivalries and better control the situation. They had to make sure that these newly appointed models will not end up becoming "little bosses" in competition with the leaders already in place. The best operators, those who were recognized by their peers to have a good command of their work, were asked to leave their workstations and to place themselves at the disposal of others intending to help them solve their problems, and therefore perform better. They were welcomed as models because they had the required knowledge. Rivalries diminished. Monitored daily, average operators progressed rapidly. This increased the general average itself. The mimetic scheme gradually recovered along with optimal working conditions. The supervisors have finally found "the time".

Hierarchy, I will never say it enough, is at the service of the collectivity. As long as it is well-conceived and entrusted to the right models. In these factories, what are considered "delicate discussions" are not about technical, financial, or production matters. It is mainly related to the person as a human being. More specifically, it concerns his relationship with colleagues during the work schedule, how he is treated and motivated, and how he is engaged in a group set to fulfill, and how he progresses and develops himself.

In the case of operators who were separated from their workstations, actions have been taken to solve a new problem causing rivalry known in the business world as the versatility concept. Over the months, sometimes years, some operators, including those who initially came with severe handicaps, have shown a high interest in learning. They also had the opportunity to enlarge their knowledge spectrum in different ways. Besides the positions and functions entrusted to them, they have become versatile. A precious and rare quality that few employees can develop in organizations. It was easy to replace an absent colleague, for example, backup a team called for a temporary increase in production, ensure an unexpected order from a customer ... In final, be able to lend a helping hand from time to time.

These versatile operators were asked, informally, to help their colleagues each time as needed. Therefore, they were under obligation to give up their position temporarily, thus losing part of their performance. Dissatisfied and annoyed, they unfairly regarded themselves as "stopgap", whereas, from the supervisor's perspective, it was a recognition of their capabilities. Frustrations emerged, allowing interindividual dissonances to lead to rivalries among people. Complaints and gossips became more and more frequent, creating an intolerable work atmosphere. "Why do you always ask me to move from my post, and never ask my colleagues?"

To reduce the tensions, several formations have been put in place. On the one hand for the supervisors, to help them look at the operators with a positive eye through active and caring pedagogy. On the other hand, to satisfy the anxious operators who felt abused, a project was initiated with a laboratory of neurosciences in Angers, the GRENE (research group in neurosciences and education). The mission of this group is to conduct research in neuroscience and education to help both the supervisors and the operators, understand how the brain functions and evolves, and how it is made to learn throughout life.

Versatility derives from a special capability that only a happy few can enjoy. It is accompanied by educational measures intended to explain that versatility is an asset and one of the most important ways for advancement. However, this versatility also allows people to open their minds and their hearts to others through mutual help, stirred up by the desire to support each other whenever needed. Thus, the managerial challenge was fulfilled since it contributed to creating the said desire. This critical issue arises with acuity today in a growing number of organizations where employees are asked to multi-task. Two or three decades ago, a single-task job was the rule.

As a matter of fact, in a shop, the cashier was never asked to display products on the shelves, and in a company, the typist would never have imagined being entrusted with the phone switchboard. This is no longer the case today. The new rules under which versatility has been established often remained unsaid. The accumulation of things left unrevealed at all levels in the organization has contributed to creating stress and frustrations. A situation that could have been easily avoided. Formalize, prioritize, say what is useful; create the desire to fit in, and then progress.

Cedric was in this situation. On his entry to the factory, in 1999, he admits that he spends a long time learning. Sometimes in vain. His trainers might have been tempted to give up on him or leave him alone. On the contrary, they preferred to keep trying, heartily, by repeating the same gesture in front of him, and then explaining to him how useful this small gesture was for him and the rest of the chain and, more broadly, for the entire factory. By working with constant application, he finally developed his abilities and understood the value of his work. He learned to assemble the wires following different diagrams, then how to use the cutting machines, how to control the quality of finished products, how to manage the warehouse, and how to use a computer, which initially was difficult. Then, by practicing and executing these various tasks, he became a perfect versatile employee.

This versatility was the outcome of a smart combination of different tasks. When Cédric is not present at his workstation, in the capacity of an operator, or at the production line, he is performing as a versatile worker at different stations, or as a training assistant. In the latter case, Cedric is also involved in the training of newcomers and even colleagues. He cultivated a desire that is, for him, the source of immense satisfaction.

Carry out the training and be sure that its "trainee students" succeed to put learning into practice. "That means I'm a good trainer," he told me, blooming with pride. He did not forget the difficulties he encountered while learning. His mission is fulfilled through the transmission of learning. It's the case of all good masters, of all good professors. Their happiness lies in their willingness and ability to teach the pupils and share their knowledge and know-how. Without being jealous.

Cédric feels that he now exists. He considers himself valuable. He would not have been if he had stayed at home, surviving with a handicap. He brings this added value to the factory, but the factory also brings him what I call the fundamental right to fulfillment and why not self-actualization. Thanks to his salary, he was able to become independent. Today he is having a relationship.

73

CHAPTER 7

THE REWARDS OF EFFORT

Charles' arrival at the factory was a challenge. One more challenge. Severely bipolar, he had for many years alternated long phases of intense excitement with periods of deep depression. He was frequently hospitalized in the psychiatric section where chemical treatments were administered to stabilize his mood, cutting him off from all inner momentum. As a last resort, they had directed him towards the world of work. One last chance before another hospitalization – inevitable, according to his doctors.

I met him for the first time at the factory in Le Mans where he worked. Except for a very slight stiffness, and although he was not a fluent speaker, nothing in his conversation indicated that he was disabled Nor would anything have led me to imagine that he was continuing his chemical treatment. His medications were in the form of a bimonthly injection plus daily pills which, when administered in the hospital, unfortunately, turn the patient into a vegetable, prostrate on a chair until being taken back to bed.

At the factory, Charles had, from the beginning, set himself some objectives and was constantly very demanding. He became stronger, progressing as he settled into the routine of professional life. He clung to his work, and he quickly understood that it was the only way out for him. He was conscious of the importance of each new step taken, and wanted to move forward.

Trading a disabled adult allowance for the benefit of a regular wage was perceived as a great victory. Further, being able to rent his own apartment was another achievement. Thus, did he succeed to escape from an environment that was toxic to him, even unintentionally? It's possible. He was quite satisfied with his new life, "without interference or limitations to consider", as he says. He strove to take care of himself. He started cleaning, tidying up, shopping for groceries, and washing the dishes. He discovered he had a passion for new technologies, the podcasts of the soul, and radio programs he listens to after work when he has time. Basically, he discovered a new dimension: the "work culture".

At the factory, he kept on trying his utmost. They promoted him to the position of supervisor. Since his arrival, he was no longer regarded as disabled; he stopped looking at himself as a disableded person. Finally stabilized, he gained self-confidence. He rebuilt himself.

When I saw Charles a few months later, he had left the AMIPI learning factory, where he had spent a year and a half. He is now working just a few kilometers away, in a "normal" work environment. It is a delivery company, a sort of small-scale Amazon. He collects small dimension products in a vast warehouse and prepares packages for shipping along with the necessary documents. He succeeded in what we commonly call here the path of insertion.

It was just after Christmas; he was proud to have held up despite the intense flow of deliveries throughout the month of December. A tutor had been assigned to him, whose presence is reassuring even if Charles needs to consult him less. Fully integrated into his new team, Charles recognizes that he is doing a lot of effort in socialization during work. Further, in break periods, when he joins his colleagues to chat and relax, he completely forgets about his disability and becomes "a normal guy, like all others". Still, Charles sometimes suffers, because of the effects of the treatment, like muscle fatigue, cramps, and stiffness. Despite all the inconveniences he does not really care. He remains motivated and perseveres because he likes his new job and because he is happy. "I have made progress in life; I now have a status."

Charles had made friends at AMIPI. He is proud to return regularly in the evening, after work, to tell them about his new life. Unwittingly, he became their role model. Quentin, the site coordinator of the AMIPI Foundation (the equivalent of an industrial director) regrets his departure. He had "lost a good one", as he said. But, at the same time, he is proud of the factory that made Charles autonomous and operational. He encourages Charles' visits to his former colleagues. He knows that these visits will speed up the integration process that is dear to his heart. More specifically, the path from "learning" factories into so-called "normal" factories. Charles is hereafter the role model who tells the operators: "I did it, just do it by imitating me. Now you are ready." He liberates them from the fear of change by motivating them with desire. But every desire is mimetic, and therefore contagious.

Each year, about fifteen operators move away, leaving their handicap behind, thanks to their eagerness to work and their iron will to go on with their life. This transformation allowed them to improve, to progress, to go beyond mental or intellectual disability based on their strengths and their intelligence, whatever form it takes. However, diving into the real world still frighten some people. The exemplarity of the elders - considered virtuous models - is the best pedagogy to demystify integration. The interdividuality does, as always, wonders...

Learning factories are not very different from the so-called "normal" ones. Admittedly, most employees there suffer from disabilities, but the management systems and procedures to manage human and industrial resources are identical to the ones of so-called "normal" factories. The strengths and weaknesses of each person are undoubtedly exacerbated there. Therefore, it appears that an anxious character is extremely anxious, a shy person is very shy, but a quick person is notably quick. Further, a temperament that is considered patient like that of Patrice, allows him to exult, day after day, even in a task in which the repetitiveness might seem unbearable to others. Still, for years, Patrice has been coming to work every morning with a smile on his face...

Many of these employees have had a difficult career path, sometimes even toilsome because of their disability. They have experienced exclusion or overprotection, and often jeers and admonitions that have deeply stigmatized them. Besides the endless days of doing nothing, the bitter feeling of being always perceived as "different" was grievously lived in the flesh. Therefore, their strong desire to integrate, to normalize their lives, is quite significant. At their working station, they immediately realize that they will achieve this normalization through hard work. This assertion seems to be valid for any worker: we all have our minor neuroses, some anxieties, some fears, and worries and we know well, from experience, that the "immersion into work" gradually helps in freeing ourselves from all these problems.

Their other peculiarity is transparency. Here, there are no innuendos in human relationships, no mistrust (let's assume) regarding bosses or colleagues. No lies, but an atmosphere that is marked by spontaneity. Unfortunately, the latter is now lost in most so-called "normal" work environments. As such, interdividuality is established with much more fluidity. Exchanges between models (at all levels) and learners are therefore more constructive. Because when trust is established, despite minor disputes, rivalries disappear.

In an "ordinary" work environment, it has become usual for an employee to complain because he is at work, considering it a forced duty, a sort of necessary misfortune. Further, it has become common to dream of vacations and claim it loudly. They are locked into the "prison of the mind", as Maurice Vendre said. They reproduce a representation of what work is which does not really help build oneself.

On the opposite, when this same employee finds himself unemployed, he dreams only of work, being then fully aware of what disabled workers already know. Work does not only allow one to fulfill his or her basic needs; it does more: it contributes to the building of oneself. Therefore, work is simply a springboard helping to exist and to become.

It is not a coincidence that those who have experienced exclusion in one form or another, such as disability, long-term sick leave, unemployment, etc. develop and nourish a certain need to make an effort in the intent to fulfill themselves, and stabilize their life. They have encountered a different way and representation of what it means to work, a new opportunity. Their motivation is priceless for any organization!

Another remarkable fact deserves to be analyzed: the therapeutic value of effort and work. On the one hand, statistics show that despite absenteeism rates, people who have a job are often less sick than those who are unemployed and spend their days at home doing nothing. On the other hand, work heals.

This truth could be applied to all. As a matter of fact, I had the opportunity to confirm it when I would listen to patients complaining of various physical, psychological, conjugal, and social problems. They found themselves spontaneously on their way to remission as soon as a useful goal was given to their lives, with all the constraints, demands, and schedules to respect. Issues that are bound to happen in normal life.

In this respect, I have seen many of my comrades retiring. I have thoroughly observed them. Because of the lack of activity, they are depressed and get sick. This was typically the case with my notary, who suddenly developed devastating cancer. He died, six months after the termination of his activities.

In a learning factory, this reality is quite spectacular. I will cite Joseph's case. His disability appeared a few months after his birth. His gestures were uncoordinated, often unintentionally. His psychometric problems were then confirmed at the age of two. His doctors diagnosed a syndrome of Kabuki. However, despite the growth hormones which were prescribed for him, he could not adapt to school, and hung out in a few specialized institutions, with no notable achievements. In addition, what worsened the situation is that his parents resolutely considered him useless, pretending that he would never be able to do anything with his life but wait for time to pass.

However, the promise of employment at the AMIPI learning factory in Nantes - in the automobile sector, which required a great manual skillfulness - has left his parents disoriented and confused. As a matter of fact, during the first days, Joseph could not coordinate his gestures in order to properly roll up the cables and coil them on themselves. He, unfortunately, rolled up his hands instead, making knots with his arms. He was afraid and constantly shaking, and his lack of self-confidence was very apparent. A case that seemed totally hopeless...

His role model was an assistant operator who had herself gone through a very similar learning scheme and who showed infinite patience, repeating untiringly the gesture that he had to accomplish and accompanying him until he finally succeeded. At one time, Joseph said laughing: I was the first to be stupefied by the results.

He caught himself in the challenging game of learning, attempting to learn more and more, tirelessly. With each new activity and task he succeeds, gains self-confidence, and becomes more eager to continue. And fortunately, without additional chemical treatment, his gestures become increasingly precise. Intrigued by his son's progress and amazing development, the mother came to visit the factory. She happily discovered that it was a real factory and that his son was up to many challenges, meeting all the job requirements...

Three years later, Joseph was appointed training assistant. He now teaches the rules of the profession and untiringly shows the precise gestures to newcomers. He passes his driver's license. He leaves his parents and settle down in his home, in his own apartment. He knows that Kabuki syndrome is still present in his body, but he can control it and has just embarked on an activity that was previously unimaginable for him: bodybuilding. During his last months at the factory, they classified him among the brightest elements. Since our encounter, he succeeded integrating himself into a "normal" company. He is now working as a manager at Leroy Merlin. A position that allows him to be in direct contact with customers.

Joseph healed by patiently learning and self-appropriating gestures. He made considerable efforts to coordinate the movement of his hands and his arms. Accordingly, new synapses between neurons were created, strengthening areas of the brain that could palliate his weaknesses. He is fully conscious of the situation: "I understood the need to make an effort after my first success, when I managed to wrap wires without making a mistake. Then, I realized that I was on the path to remission. Today, I can confirm that I overcame my disability because of persistence and hard work".

His recovery lies not in the absence of visual symptoms. For him, it was because of the opportunity to reintegrate into the social and professional world. Simply, to come out of isolation.

CHAPTER 8

THE FACTORIES OF BEING

Tomorrow promises to be a tragedy for human kind.

Tomorrow, we are told, work will be reserved for an elite: creative people, artists, intellectuals, decision-makers, a few senior executives and very skillful technicians. For all the others, forced to give up on their job because more efficient and less expensive robots will replace them, a universal salary will be paid, assuming that states still have the possibility to provide it.

Tomorrow, if we are not careful, the GAFAM, the American digital giant composed of Google, Apple, Facebook, Amazon, and Microsoft, along with their Chinese counterpart the BATX composed of Baidu, Alibaba, Tencent, and Xiaomi, will replace Homo Faber, the man who produces. The same human who emerged from prehistoric times by inventing fire and then tools, that human who kept improving these tools to forge civilizations over centuries, he who, by manufacturing, consecrated humanity and perfected it, thus making himself.

What will happen to this Homo Faber if, tomorrow, it stops producing? If lands and factories are empty of farmers and workers? if, in hospitals, doctors and nurses are replaced by robots, if we even put aside having a profession, and/or simply stop learning?

Aren't political talks deliberately preparing us for this eventuality? They consistently and massively offer to us at all levels the opportunity to take things for granted - effortless, easier, and still easier. In the same line of thought, they consider effort, such as work and school, an unbearable duty and a punishment. Focusing more particularly on assistance and subventions, these political tasks encourage large parts of the population to stop making any effort. Such observation is unfortunately promoted not only to people suffering from disabilities but also to the most deprived, the most disadvantaged, and the least educated. Instead of motivating them to face their problems, to react, stand up and help themselves. Rather than revealing the truth to them by loudly claiming that work is the solution and an award by itself. These people are regrettably told instead: "Wait for help and ask for it."

If he no longer produces, the human being will cease to recreate himself. If he stops cutting stones, his own inner stone will lie fallow. Because, beyond its productive aspect, which includes transforming the substance and its surrounding environment, work has an initiatory aspect. For me, this initiation is even more important. This is possible through progressive transformation under the guidance of a master. Work shapes the individual, and builds him, allowing him to move forward, to exist.

A factory, a business, or a trade has a mission which is to create quality products, besides developing the brains of those who make them. The more they develop brains, the better the products! I will give one example: The London taxis. London is a very large city with a little over 25 000 streets. To obtain their license, and then be able to convey passengers to their destination, London taxi drivers have for decades had to memorize the names of these streets and all the connections between them. On the MRIs, we clearly saw that in the brain of most experienced drivers, an area next to the hippocampus has enriched itself, over the years, improving intelligence because of good practice. However, since the existence of the GPS and geolocation devices, this effort of memorization no longer needs to be made. Consequently, the brain is no longer required to develop the new synapses that were essential to accomplish its task. As a result, the famous brains of London taxi drivers (famous in that they had been the subject of numerous studies!) have unfortunately become common place...

Work allows human being to become someone instead of being nothing. Car robots will soon replace these drivers. Same for the trucks, trains, buses, or planes. A question remains. What will happen to these drivers and pilots? There is no doubt that new professions which are unknown today will emerge and develop over the years. Will they be the future professions for everyone? No one dares to confirm it. Furthermore, no one so far pretends to believe it.

I have for a long time freely walked around the AMIPI factory premises. A question often came to my mind which is addressed to the operators, while they were concentrating on their tasks: "Are you happy to work here? » Billy, Cedric,

Jeanne, Diane, and all the others answered me with a plain-spoken yes. It is a no-doubt yes.

Patrice, in charge of the warehouse and logistics at the Le Mans factory, insists: "I wake up at 6 a.m. every morning, and I come to work with a big smile. Before working, I got bored staying at home. Now, here, I take care of myself and, amazingly, I don't notice the time passing. Here also, there are friends. And then, there is a third essential thing: I am happy because people trust me, I do my job properly and my bosses know I am performing well. It's hard when we have experienced exclusion. When we aren't trusted, it's simply death."

What Patrice gains here and what he experiences is self-confidence and trust in others. It is about mutual respect and self-respect as well. When he comes to work, he respects himself. If he stays at home doing nothing, he loses his self-respect. In addition, this trust and respect cannot be valued in terms of Euros. This respect gave him the opportunity, month after month, to rebuild himself and to grow and become someone thoughtful. His reward, at the end of his days of work, is what the continuous effort allowed him to become. More specifically, to be.

The day robots take over our jobs and when there will be no more factories, we will have to reinvent them. The factories of tomorrow, where men and women will work for the beauty of the work itself. They may no longer produce goods or wealth, but they will produce men capable of being.

Should we recommence building new cathedrals? Should we inaugurate factories dedicated to the embellishment of green spaces? Should we invent new products to be manufactured by humans? Should we remove robots from work so that Homo Faber survives? Without any doubt, there will be a little bit of all this.

It is also an economic imperative: helping companies financially, by allocating resources in order to support jobs sustainability. This will definitely cost less to the State than the payment of a universal income or unemployment allowances. For the AMIPI learning factories alone, the generated cost of non-public expenditure is around 18 million euros per year.

What are we all waiting for to work?

CHAPTER 9

Dialogue between the scientist and the entrepreneur

JEAN-MICHEL OUGHOURLIAN

AND JEAN-MARC RICHARD:

MIMETIC PSYCHOLOGY IN ACTION

Professor Jean-Michel Oughourlian is the "father" of mimetic psychology, a metapsychology, that is to say a global system for understanding psychic processes and their interactions. A theory he confirmed through his neuroscientific works on mirror neurons and on the impact of mimetism on our daily lives, and which he applied in his long psychiatric practice.

Both in the hospital and in practice, the results have been spectacular: by thinking differently about the individual, that is to say, by considering him only in relation to others, in what he called interdividuality, he soothed suffering, overcame handicaps, and saved those who were considered irredeemable.

Jean-Marc Richard is the president of the AMIPI Foundation and forefather of implementing the work of Professor Oughourlian in a new field: the business world. He was imbued with this work after reading Professor

Oughourlian's shocking book, "Our Third Brain," and, in agreement with the directors of AMIPI, integrated it into the operation of the UPAIs, the foundation's learning factories. The notions of models, rivalry, desire, and authority, associated with an active and benevolent pedagogy oriented towards success, have led to an interesting result: an increase in productivity that was associated with a spectacular development of "makers" – employees, among more than 80% suffer from a cognitive handicap.

Can this approach be exported -- i.e., extended to all companies, or even to the whole society? A dialogue between two enlightened men...

- Let's start with the basics. What is a model in mimetic psychology, and how can this concept be transposed into the world of business without being distorted?

Jean-Michel Oughourlian - Based on different studies on mirror neurons, science has now fully demonstrated that our brains are mimically constituted. The imitation of appearance, of having, of being and of desiring, that is to say, the "movement towards" the other, considered a model, is almost obligatory. From there, two lines of thought are considered:

1/The responsibility of the model.

Parents, teachers, business leaders, hierarchical superiors, political leaders, all those who are imposed as models, (that is, not "chosen") must become aware, of the important responsibility of their behavior, being the models from which we are inspired and which we imitate.

2/The choice of a model. In what is, in fact, a mimetic obligation, the space of freedom that is left to us is, at a certain moment of the development, the choice of a model, or even models. Those who are satisfied with a single model are called "fanatics." Most individuals, fortunately, know how to take, throughout their existence, different models that combine in the intent to create a patchwork which will constitute us. Further, each patchwork, that is to say each individual, is original, singular, not in each of its parts (which all result from imitation), but in the way these different parts are composed together.

Jean-Marc Richard - The question is about knowing how we address, in a factory or in a company, these two fundamental dimensions: that of the scope of responsibility of the model and that of the choice of the model. As a matter of fact, a role model is not appointed by decree. If I tell someone, "You are going to be a role model," he will be tempted to take advantage of this role to gain influence over others, and there will be an abuse of power. Moreover, no one can impose himself as a model.

This initiative is doomed to failure because everyone can freely choose which model to follow. On the other hand, our responsibility as business leaders or bosses is to create conditions that allow models to emerge at all levels.

There are two questions that I systematically ask those who work in our factories. First: "Who is leading you?" Then: "Who are the role models you learn from?" I help them become aware of the identity of their role models. AMIPI is an operational organization, therefore experimental, whose purpose is the development of people and then their integration into an ordinary environment. It is therefore necessary to create the appropriate conditions for this experiment.

- You both focus on the notion of desire. It is not spontaneously associated with the idea of work. Is desire necessary? Therefore, how do you create it in the case of someone who lacks desire?

J-M. Oughourlian - Desire is mimetic. For a desire to be triggered in me, I must see it in action in someone else. There is no other solution. A teacher who loves what he teaches will transmit, along with knowledge, the desire to seek this knowledge. And this is valid for everything: advertising, education, learning, and life as a whole are based on this principle. It is the desire for the action itself that motivates one to imitate, as well as the act that it has generated. In sports, this is called "training." To train someone is to create in him a desire and to incite him to compete positively with me.

J-M. Richard - We are manufacturers; we don't live in the world of "Care Bears". When we try to find his or her own professional vocation in each of our employees, it is also for reasons of enhanced performance and outcomes. By awakening his desire, we will help him to learn, to train, to develop, and to grow. More broadly, we have understood that it is necessary to take into consideration the interaction factor, that is, human beings' relationships with one another, without precluding the idea of profitability in order to survive. This does not necessarily exclude the confrontations for which we have established a framework: the "sensitive discussion". This allows you to talk about the state of affairs and to raise the points of dispute at a determined time and space, in the presence of a mediator. In three years, thanks to the contributions of mimetic psychology and mirror neurons, we have increased our yields by 5%. Operators in our factories are individually monitored in terms of production metrics and level of quality. Also, the financial challenges are real. As a matter of fact, a 1% return represents 100,000 euros in additional earnings. And we have not deviated from our mission: at AMIPI, the same activity must simultaneously develop an individual's brain and a product simultaneously.

- Can your company serve as a model for others?

J-M. Richard - A company is like a brain: it needs the contribution of many. However, if we start pretending to be a model, others will perceive us as rivals, which is the opposite of the role of a model. The AMIPI Foundation evolves in a free market economic system since it manufactures and sells products. I consider that the presence of entrepreneurs is essential to the economy of a country, but most of the time, I will not tell others what they have to do and how to do it. I admit, however, that the fact of sharing our experience and know-how has allowed our operators to easily integrate traditional companies into regular market conditions with excellent scores (this was the case for 28 of our operators in 2021). These successful results have positioned us as a model that "works".

- You also both insist on the importance of "doing". Is it the same when it comes to directing?

J-M. Oughourlian - The French tradition consists first of learning the theory at school, then trying to apply it in business when you have no experience of the implementation process yet. Those who arrive in this context, by being perceived as "knowledgeable", automatically create a rivalry with those who are there and who possess real "knowledge." A hospital director who takes up his new position should first go to the stretcher-bearers, the nurses, the caregivers, those who "do", and then start making decisions. Great business leaders, those who created dynasties, started at the bottom of the ladder and gradually moved up. They are aware of all levels of the hierarchy and understand that decisions made at the highest levels should never be the only solutions to problems that arise at the lowest levels.

J-M. Richard - François Michelin said: "Knowledgeable people are needed, but we give them three years to 'land'." You don't learn to drive a vehicle in a book, and, as the professor says, the evolution of the brain is only possible by "doing". This phrase has become the motto of our learning factories.

J-M. Oughourlian - Some of my former colleagues, upon retirement, decided to interrupt all activities to devote their time to leisure and travel. They have stopped "doing". After the first few months, they got tired, and their desire disappeared and died out. They were no longer driven by a goal. At home, we systematically examine ourselves, especially when we are doctors. We end up finding "things". You know this sentence from Doctor Knock, in "Knock or the Triumph of Medicine", the play by Jules Romains: "Any healthy man is a sick person who does not know he is." These new retirees found illnesses that they sometimes actually fall ill with. Those who have continued to have a professional activity, regardless of whether it is paid or not (and I am thinking here of the associative field), have kept their bodies agile and their minds alert. It is working. This statement applies to everyone. When you stay at home, benefiting from allocations, the cost of unemployment is very high. The isolation in which one is immersed is a form of disability and

J-M. Richard - Our factories are not hospitals, but they are nevertheless places of "care"! We do not know the disabilities of our operators; we only know that they are recognized as disabled workers. In this regard, we have implemented two principles. On the one hand, we stay alert to continuously check that they are producing quality work, quality behavior, and knowing how to live decently, without, however, always being by their side. Furthermore, they have a job on which they concentrate and learn to organize themselves. On the other hand, we make sure to introduce different key learning modules, small modifications, and challenges that will continually enliven their desire to learn and succeed.

The brain remains mobilized and, thanks to its plasticity, new synapses develop and allow general progress. Our ambition, and theirs too, is then to nurture a personal and professional project, to get out of the learning factory to join -- through an internship and then on a permanent contract -- the community of so-called traditional companies that surround us and that are ready to welcome them. The progress that we see, cognitively and emotionally and even physically, would have been inconceivable without real and continuous work.

J-M. Oughourlian - We know many organizations that take care of people suffering from disabilities by affixing the label of disability to them for life. I don't see them changing their lives, making them evolve, making them learn, or simply improving them in some way. You, on the contrary, by integrating them into an appropriate structure, engaging them into activities, encouraging them to work according to their capabilities, you are making them progress and gradually integrate a regular life. Therefore, there is a difference in perspective between you and others. And a very clear difference in results that I noticed while spending long periods of time in your factories, alongside the operators!

J-M. Richard - Maurice Vendre's decision to build learning factories and to use the industrial system as a means has allowed us to improve the individual through appropriate learning that develops his faculties and his senses, then inserts him into a traditional environment. In other words, give real autonomy to the person. Studies and research have shown us that, for this purpose, all the senses and all the abilities must be called upon: the plasticity of the brain increases when the vision, hearing, touch, which is fundamental, memory, and attention, etc., are solicited at the same time. A factory operator or an apprentice cook who performs a professional task with great autonomy is called upon to mobilize more senses and more faculties, and therefore has infinitely more possibilities to progress.

- Empathy, help: how far should we go? And here, I am addressing both the neuropsychiatrist and the business manager, whose objective is also production and growth...

J-M. Richard - In AMIPI's learning factories, operators are not puppets moved by puppeteers. In other words, they are not constantly supported and helped. They are certainly more fragile than average people. However, hyper-protection would not benefit the development of their brains or the company as a whole. Indeed, hyper-protection and excess of empathy would lead us to create not ghettos but "silos", bringing together homogeneous populations in terms of disability and preventing them from communicating with society. Disabilities, when isolated or confined in a sort of silo, are scary. It develops "racism" and exclusions. I can cite many examples experienced by those who are the closest to me. If our French society were more attentive to the interests of the person, we would place most people in difficulty in companies, as soon as they have the capacity to work. Technologies are a great opportunity to compensate for their handicap and gain autonomy.

J-M. Oughourlian - Facing a case of disability, we must avoid two errors, each as fatal as the other. The first is the rejection of the other, which we get rid of by entrusting him to an institute where, often, he will not do much and will not be properly helped to develop. The second is hyper-protection: I'm not going to help the other, I'm going to do it for him; I will, in a way, reduce him. In mimetic psychology, this is called "disguised rivalry." Real empathy is the opposite of rivalry. I'll try to integrate the other by finding him something he really wants, knowing that he is not often fully aware of what he wants. This empathy is not intrusive, but benevolent. The model clearly proposes itself as a leading model and not as a rival. Instead of suffocating or imprisoning the other, the model will provide him with the means to be autonomous and move forward in his life. In other words, the model will help, but he will not replace the other. I have seen this attitude in learning factories where, in order to empower individuals, there are deliberately no educators and very few supervisors. Each has a reference, a model that he can call upon if necessary. The operator calls the line assistant, who himself calls his "boss," etc. In this hierarchy, everyone is ready to help, allowing the others to progress further. The operator does not see them as potential rivals. This is where Interdividuality works harmoniously and this is what I call real empathy, which is neither surrender nor suffocation.

J-M. Richard - However, the challenge in our factories is to keep empathy under control. Everyone should benefit from good doctors and treatment, but no one should be anchored in his disease. No one is stigmatized. This is the fight that Maurice Vendre has carried out, which scientists have come to pursue along with us. I no longer want a society of hyper-empathy or one of hyper-performance. Both cases exclude and bring families of disabled people to amplify the protections around them, believing they are helping them. While they are not. Still, I can understand their attitude, since it also reflects my personal case. But when we advocate a society that used to embrace protection, everything depends on the assistance of others.

- Concretely, Jean-Marc Richard, how do you do it?

J-M. Richard - My key word is controlled empathy: going towards the other and understanding him, but controlling the relationship in the interest of both parties. In this condition, there can be empathy in the workplace. I accompanied, among others, a young man who was said to be fearful, who was not very successful in his studies, and who was developing anxieties. A psychic fragility had been diagnosed by the psychiatrist who was treating him. For his parents, following our discussions, the hospital was not a solution. They did not want him to be more anchored in his problem, if this was really the case. They seriously raised the issue with him and took charge by asking him to abandon his university curriculum, a source of so many worries for him. They then helped him find his desire, that is to say, in this case, his professional vocation, a goal that he could himself carry and achieve, in order to have more chances to succeed. As I often say to our employees who lead, choose a good goal. If it is too ambitious or not ambitious enough, it is not good. To come back to this young man, his studies were a way to relieve himself. They helped his brain develop and he gradually stopped being anxious. He passes his exams and his internships and knows that he will have a job that he will enjoy. The rest followed. He now has a girlfriend, maintains a constant relationship with his doctor, and follows a minimal treatment plan. He is fulfilled because his parents stopped bringing him to them, to their role model, but went to him. By infantilizing, we destroy. Without the experience of AMIPI, would I have succeeded in helping these families to change their view of their own children? How many failures and disasters could have been avoided if these testimonies had reached the greatest number of people prior to the irreversible crisis?

J-M. Oughourlian - Your empathy was to guide them to a way out. This is also what you do in your factories where the exit door is special: it is the integration of people with disabilities into a so-called classical environment. This empathy, which is not hyper-empathy, leads you not to keep them because they need to be protected, but to lead them elsewhere, as you did for this young man!

J-M. Richard - At AMIPI, we have abandoned work medals, which reward longevity in a company, in favor of integration medals, which encourage mobility. For us, the hero is not the one who stays, but the one who leaves. Our society fears mobility; because of my temperament, immobility frightens me. What more will you learn after a few years in the same position at the same company? But when you stop learning, you regress. The real challenge in business is not whether you are rich or not, because you can die rich. It is to know if we are alive and if our brain is alert, therefore keeps learning.

Another theme dealt with which is central to mimetic psychology is that of the relationship between power and authority. This subject is just as important in an organization!

J-M. Oughourlian - Let's start by explaining the idea. Simply put, power is exercised from the top down and authority is invested from the bottom up. One cannot impose one's authority as one imposes one's power: I confer authority on my master if I consider that he knows better than me, and I then set him up as a model. On the other hand, a person who has power but not knowledge in the field concerned can impose his point of view on me. He will then exercise his power, not his authority. In general, when we take someone as a model, we give him authority, even if he does not have power. On the other hand, rivalries are set up when those who have power do not have authority. I will give you an example: I can exercise my power and order you to open your umbrella at the next crossroads. To carry out this order, you will have to remember what I have told you during your journey. On the other hand, if I suggest that you open it, despite the sun, and if I have the authority to convince you to do it, you will mimically execute what I have suggested to you. By opening the umbrella, you will even think that it was you who took the initiative.

J-M. Richard - The notions of power and authority can become the poison of a collective action. In our factories, the heads of groups or of sections are not parachuted in from the outside; they are extracted from the group when the others confer authority on them, take them as a model, consider them as a reference, or designate them as someone who knows better than they know. Céline, who is part of our training team, had a sentence that we use on a daily basis: "If you force me, I oppose; if you explain things to me, I get involved."

J-M. Oughourlian - Leaders are thus promoted by stepping out of line and having understood all the mechanisms of the machine. It is the selection method used by Napoleon, who chose his marshals not from those who graduated from the schools of war but from those who had extensive battleground experience. Thus, the best horsemen, the best artillerymen, and the best shooters became captains, then generals, then marshals of France. They were real role models.

J-M. Richard - Inspired by your works, Professor, I have implemented managerial and governance processes based on a few key concepts that can be extended to all companies:

1) Build assertive leadership in well-identified areas, working with everyone on their own intentions (these are the ports of arrival).

2) Fight against sterile rivalries by integrating the principles of mimicry: the model (the teacher) must adopt a posture of transmission to remain a model. To do this, we systematically need to favor trios over duos; arbitration is always necessary and avoids dominant-dominated relationships.

3) Implement the collective intelligence that is built through interdividuality.

4) Initiate the concept of "wanting something", therefore creating the notion of desire, which is the only guarantee of the durability of learning.

5) Foster controlled empathy, which encourages collective action while also allowing employees to progress toward greater freedom, independence, and responsibility.

All our work consists of allowing the emergence of real models, namely competent, benevolent, and willing to transmit knowledge. All this while collectively managing the poison of rivalry.

- You both agree on the fact that work is an imperative, not only to find housing and food, but almost to exist. However, we know that there is not enough work for all: some are forced into unemployment. What can we tell them?

J-M. Richard - I sincerely believe that the end of labor is not inevitable. Under certain conditions, of course. Thus, organizations and individuals should be more engaged in Corporate Social and Environmental Responsibility, in the objective of creating or repatriating work in France. Let's build factories. Let's reconnect with what I call the "duality of work," which means succeeding, at the same time, in making good products and developing people's brains. In exchange for this effort made by the companies, the State could consider significant reductions in charges. He would have everything to gain from it: if we succeed in returning people to the classical production system, they will not only cost him nothing (because they will have income, start consuming again, paying taxes, and so on). Further, work is a prerequisite of harmoniously being able to live together.

J-M. Oughourlian - It is important to clarify the difference between work and employment. To characterize it, I would say that work is the mistress for whom we multiply our efforts and whom we want to see, while employment is the lifelong marriage contract that gets bogged down in routines. Employment is what feeds a person; work is what develops it. It is a desire, a passion, a commitment. Employment is a contract; the work involves efforts to keep alive what initially made up the soul of the contract. It is not contractual but leads to a permanent desire to invest himself and to perform. It is a self-powered machine; an individual enthusiastic about his work does not count the hours. One could not have told Picasso to stop painting because he had exceeded 35 hours per week. A responsible government must indeed find a way to maintain employment, otherwise we will only produce disabled people in the sense that I understand it, that is to say, isolated people, cut off from life.

J-M. Richard - The industrial system represents a real opportunity to create and secure jobs in the sense that you indicate and therefore becomes a real vector of integration for the most vulnerable populations. 25% of German employees work in industry, a growing sector there, while in France, for decades, industrial jobs have disappeared. However, the Germans had collectively consented to maintain competitiveness without scarifying people as the adjustment variable.

This battle for the overall competitiveness of the industrial system, which must always compare the overall cost of work with that of non-work, is the only battle that is worthwhile. I will introduce some key figures: An AMIPI factory receives state aid equivalent to 14,000 euros per year and per person. It pays the same amount in VAT and charges, which means that it costs nothing to the State. At the same time, a long-term unemployed person costs the State an average of 30,000 euros per year, all aid combined. The calculation is quickly made: since our factories cost nothing, the difference at the expense of the State is 30,000 euros, and when we integrate our operators into traditional companies, the savings for the State are much higher. In view of these figures, a shutdown of our factories would represent a public expenditure of 27 million euros every year (900 employees x 30,000 euros), 270 million euros over ten years. On a larger scale, 500,000 additional unemployed people have an overall annual cost for the State of 15 billion euros per year, or 150 billion euros over ten years. This is the main reason that incited the Germans, but also the Swiss, to think and organize themselves differently to face the negative effects of globalization.

By dint of not seizing the tremendous opportunity that work, particularly manufacturing and craftsmanship, represent for developing a society and, in addition, creating wealth, we keep suffering from mass unemployment where very few solutions are offered and where public spending increases every year. The younger generations are often unaware of these facts and "working in the factory" is still considered by the traditional school system as a last solution. This book also aims to enlighten all our educators and make them want to explore other avenues. The other hypothesis that the Foundation wishes to promote with the ministries concerned, the active forces, and the unions, is to encourage the industrial system to develop learning factories in France. At AMIPI, the production of the operators is of high quality, and the productivity is constantly improving.

In addition, this system has the merit of never considering people as machines, performing only repetitive tasks over very long periods of time. For us, learning, when designed according to the methods developed by Maurice Vendre and his team, is a source of development of synaptic connections, as Professor Kandel, who won the Nobel Prize in Medicine in 2000, demonstrated. It is incredible to imagine that, in the 1960s, Maurice Vendre, by his own intuition and with the constant support of Professor Robert Debré, was able to demonstrate this. The challenge for our society is the preservation of social peace; the quality of life in a country can be improved through this dual work that reconciles product development and the development of the person's abilities. "You have to succeed; they have no choice", Maurice Vendre told me on his hospital bed in Cholet, shortly before his death in 2014. It was a message of hope. I am convinced that everything is still possible.

(comments collected by Djénane Kareh Tager)

AMIPI, A MISSION

By Maryse Vendre

Co-founder of AMIPI

History can be summarized by a famous comment byGeneral De Gaulle while visiting the Ecole Polytechnique: "The most difficult thing isn't getting out of Polytechnique; it's getting out of the   ordinary".

To Maurice, the founder of AMIPI, who made us grow up, who inspired us with his creative mind and his belief in human capabilities that generate progress and development through the intelligent progressive process of learning, all types of learning.

To Pascale Toscani, Research Director at the Angers Neuroscience Laboratory, who helped us develop a system allowing our operators to become aware of their aptitudes and create their own personal development.
To Doctor Pamela Banta-Lavenex who is carrying out a study with us on the different memories of intellectually disabled people (a world first) and who recognizes our scientific pedagogy as a precious element in the development of people.
All three made us stand out from the crowd,
And of course, Professor Jean-Michel Oughourlian, whose mimetic psychology was turned into an account by Jean-

Marc Richard to enlighten and transform the management of the Foundation.

"Stupid he is, stupid he will remain. What can you do?" How many times have I heard these words? And how many times have I confirmed that it is fundamental nonsense?

On December 23rd, 1954, a long-awaited baby was born with an additional chromosome 21. The situation is highly critical and extremely painful for his parents, Maurice and Michèle Vendre.

Bernard is a child almost like the others, with some issues: delays in the formation of the teeth, normal walking, a tongue too thick that needs sensitive surgery that will facilitate language.

At four years old, he entered kindergarten despite the hesitation and resistance of some parents, who were worried about the effects of this relationship for their child. The director of the school disregarded these apprehensions and concerns. Children behave with him as with any other child. With his parents, he plays. All is play and solicitation. Little by little, the games are diversifying and becoming more complex. He's making progress.

Further, the level of primary school is insurmountable. We are in 1960. Bernard is 6 years old; the director of the school is quite firm: "He will not be able to follow the preparatory course. Reading and counting will be out of his reach. We can no longer do anything more for him." The sentence is accompanied by a letter. The child is returned to his parents.

A doctor specialized in trisomy 21 is consulted in Paris. He confirms: "Your son will always be an idiot, or at best a fool, so there is nothing you can do about it." This was what medicine was capable to teach at the end of the 1950s. An article in Le Monde, dating from 1958, even supported it.

However, Maurice Vendre was not convinced. He believed that evolution is possible and has had proof over the past six years: if Bernard has some difficulties decoding the messages he receives, perhaps there is a malfunction that can be repaired in the decoding system? At that time, the idea seemed completely far-fetched, the "people who know" have always said that there was nothing to do.

Facing such a situation, Maurice Vendre, who was then a director of a bank branch, rolled up his sleeves and decided to create an association, the ADAPEI of Maine-et-Loire. (a departmental association to assist parents with disabled children). The main idea consists of opening a specialized school for children suffering from intellectual disabilities, whether they have Down syndrome or not. At that time, the only existing establishments were "asylums" often called nurseries (they were aptly named: children were kept there since nothing could be done for them).

Accordingly, the first IMP (Médico-pedagogical institute) was born in 1961, in Cholet, offering a special educational program inspired by Montessori methods, calling on the education of all the senses, including the kinesthetic sense that was mostly neglected. The objective was clear: the emulation of children to give them confidence and, ultimately, to allow them to evolve along a normal path.

By seeing all these children progress, Maurice Vendre becomes fully aware of the importance of the plasticity of the brain and of all the different evolutionary opportunities for people suffering from cognitive disorders. The results were indeed spectacular.

Something is happening in Cholet. Desperate parents come from different cities, asking Maurice to help their children. The reputation of the first center is growing and other IMPs are starting to emerge in Saumur, Baugé, La Pommeraye-sur-Loire, and Segré.

Educational research teams are set up. I joined the adventure in 1965 in Saumur. As a young teacher, life circumstances (and available positions at that time!) led me to specialize in disabled children's care. I thus saw Bernard and his friends grow — in autonomy, gradually gaining some intellectual capabilities through the education of the language and the senses, then the transition to pre-calculation and pre-reading, and finally through calculation and reading (for those who were able to progress), in addition to manual skills and sport.

When Bernard and his friends passed the age of the IMPs (14 years old), the AAMIPI (Association of material and intellectual assistance to disabled people) was created by Maurice and his first wife to install the IMPro (Médico-professional institute ready to cater to the needs of 14–18-year-old people). Bernard and all the others needed to pursue their learning and progress.

The first IMPro was inaugurated in 1965. While continuing to follow general education courses and practice psychomotor and sports exercises, teenagers began a professional apprenticeship such as painting, masonry, plumbing, tailoring, upkeep of premises, upkeep of linens, as well as how to make a phone call, filling out a sickness card, behaving at the table, buying a train ticket...

The professionals who were hired to pass on their techniques were part of the research teams... which, at first, was not always very easy to set up. Knowing how to do it is one thing, knowing how to transmit it is another. Educational material has been prepared, oriented towards active and "benevolent" pedagogy. The main idea was not to catastrophize errors, but to consider them as a source of progress, which required a radical change of thinking and attitude. They all had one goal: to learn how to become autonomous. These teams met once a month to assess the results before printing and registering the documents at the National Library.

Bernard was part of the first group of promotions that were trained in IMPro. I remember him at that time: a proud young man, comfortable with himself, who immediately found a job in a so-called "normal" work environment: an industrial manufacturing plant of plastic materials for construction, the Nicoll factory, located in Cholet. Many of his comrades followed the same path. They gave satisfaction, happy to have ended up in a normal factory. Far from the "idiots" or "imbeciles" found in the classic systems, they were not exceptions, on the contrary. They were young and dynamic people entering the world of work, and they constituted the majority of our promotions.

For the 15 to 20% of young adults too severely disabled to follow this integration path, Maurice Vendre invented and created, in 1969, his first sheltered workshop in Cholet: a factory where the former pupils, who had become regular employees, continued to evolve through learning the know-how and building the skills to cope easily with the ordinary working world.

All the friendly and professional relations have been put to use to bring the first orders and the first customers. The Nicoll factory where Bernard worked entrusted us with the packaging of a part of its production. Simple things, but which require manual dexterity and the obligation to provide the appropriate packaging.

The work has become more complex, always needing more dexterity to systematically meet our objectives: the development of people through learning to achieve their financial and social autonomy.

Maurice wanted everyone to have "true autonomy," which, he said, is nurtured in an industrial and capitalist society through financial autonomy. However, beyond financial means, man can only find his place in society by exercising a useful activity, recognized by all, which excludes "assistantship". Maurice rejected the idea that people with a disability should only be regarded from the angle of their handicap. He also stated that such an attitude prevents any possible evolution.

Then, thanks to a Human Resources Manager at Renault, intrigued and fascinated by the approach of these workshops, came an order for electrical wiring for cars. In the first year, our workshops only had simple wiring to manufacture. When our sponsors realized that our quality was up to the required standards, and the deadlines were respected, the tasks became more complex. As a matter of fact, they entrusted us with the entire chain, from the orders of raw materials to the final product, ready to be inserted directly into cars on assembly lines at PSA Renault, Faurecia, Plastic Omnium, etc.

In language, including scientific and medical, at the time of our first "protected workshops," (our "factories") our employees were categorized by the administrative commissions as "deeply retarded," "profoundly debilitated," or "averagely debilitated." Irrecoverable people that we recuperate. We were going against the tide of the closed traditional system. Our philosophy was openness, and our only ambition was to get them out of their handicap by integrating them as much as possible into normal social and working life.

One man fully supported us. This was Professor Robert Debré, member of the Academy of Sciences, who immersed himself in our plants and affirmed in front of his peers, gathered in the assembly in 1974: "When we have the opportunity to see up close what they did, we can only be... convinced of the soundness of the doctrine and the value of the institutions they set up and the significance of their role."

This doctrine, the results of which are obvious, seems to be that of tomorrow. "

One of his students, Professor Stéphane Thieffry, deeply inspired me with his research on the hand and its functions. He had written about them in a book, "The Hand of Man" (1973), in which, unfortunately, very few people were interested. The question that intrigued me was the possibility of whether or not to develop the kinesthetic sense, which has several functions, including that of spatializing the other senses. He himself studied the development of hand activities and their impact on the transmission of information at the level of the central nervous system. It seemed obvious to me to explore this track.

During our first meeting, he confessed to me, with great simplicity: "As a doctor, I diagnose the absence of this sense, but I did not ask myself the question of how to restore it so that a person can function again". With our psychomotricity team, we strove to implement the advice he had given me.

Until 1980, the educational research teams of the IMP and IMPRo had several missions: At the beginning, strive to achieve progressions in the fields related to each mental age, then organize these progressions into annual programs that were then divided into quarterly and weekly objectives. Then, the important thing was to establish the ways and means so that each student could easily follow his own evolution path easily. It was essential that he had visual cues, in each apprenticeship, what he is aware of achieving and what remains to be learned to reach his goal.

For teenagers, boys or girls, who could not have access to "professional" apprenticeships, simple industrial jobs were sought after and set up, then more complex jobs followed. There was also a need to find a way to measure progress through these intensive labor activities, which heavily rely on the use of the hand.

We were convinced that the development of teenagers through this industrial work was possible because, as Professor Thieffry affirms in his book, the hand is marvelously equipped to collect on its surface all the impressions directly induced by the object: touching it, shaking it, or deforming it, and then transmit a sum of information to the nervous system.

"The development and maturation of the gesture," he adds, "are not capricious and variable from one subject to another." On the contrary, everything takes place according to an order, a plan, and a rhythm common to all men... provided that the environment ensures a sufficient emotional part. The successive stages are so distinct that a trained physician can estimate a child's age from his prehension mode. Based on these findings, our mission should be to find, it seemed to me, a way to measure the progress of our apprentices at each industrial workstation.

So, I was planning to work with the foreman to, on the one hand, collect the analysis of the actual work (indicating all the movements used) and then determine the need for gestural education for each movement. To this huge work (one year of creation), we had dedicated a supervisor to this industrial section. After the creation of the psycho-gestural exercises in the seven chapters listed, came the experimentation phase on all the first- and second-year apprentices of IMPro which lasted a little more than a year, in order to verify the feasibility in long term.

As with all other series of learning, we have set up an individual monitoring system, "the progress line": to "climb" up the line, we had to take into account the time spent, but also the quality of the work. For all groups, professions, or industrial category types, the important thing was to allow our apprentices to grow towards autonomy.

The objective set by the Association was in fact to bring as many apprentices as possible into the classical work environment at the end of a course of three or four years. Between 1969 and 1980, the five IMPros that we manage succeeded in their integration mission for 70 to 85% of the workforce, depending on the year. That is 1,500 young people who have joined the traditional working world.

For those who had not been able to leave because they were not ready yet, it was, therefore, necessary to specifically set up for them a different structure: these were the AP, the Protected Workshops, which, since the law of February 2005, have become Adapted Companies. For them, it was necessary to choose industrial work that was interesting enough to meet our objectives: the development of people through learning to achieve their financial and social autonomy.

To achieve this, the educational team of our training organization, which supervises all of the adapted companies, strove to:

- Identify the different work phases of each position.

- Create individual monitoring sheets for each operator for a given position.

- Include quality criteria.

The objective remains the same: the development of each individual, in addition to the acquisition of his / her autonomy.

On their arrival, the manual gestures and skills of each operator are tested to assess their strengths and weaknesses, and thus integrate them at a working station that is neither too weak, so that they do not get bored, nor too difficult, so as not to discourage them.

Their evolution has gone beyond our expectations. Some have been given positions of greater responsibility: line assistants, controllers, storekeepers, maintenance assistants, etc. These responsibilities and position titles are of great help when they join traditional companies.

In 1976, Maurice Vendre lost his wife. We continued the adventure together. Bernard, whom I considered my son, had taken off. He lived in his own apartment next to ours. He took his meals with us when he was not at work, at the theater, or at a concert with his friends.

In 1980, Maurice ceded the presidency of ADAPEI, which he had founded, and entrusted the association with the IMPs and IMPros that we had created. The reasons for his departure are not a mystery: Some members of the association did not agree with our philosophy, our desire to push their children out, towards the outside world, towards life. They were afraid and advocated a form of protectionism as harmful as exclusion. However, when they leave our home to go to a traditional environment, our operators proudly claim: "I no longer have a label!"

Bernard died in 1992 after being hit by a car. He was thirty-eight years old. He had spent nineteen years learning and another nineteen years working hard. An image stays in my mind of him sitting on the outside steps of his paternal grandparents' country lodge. He was ten years old and said: "I, Bernard Vendre, am happy!" He certainly was.

In 2005, AAMIPI became a recognized public utility foundation, the AMIPI-Bernard Vendre Foundation, which has retained the same objectives as the association from which it originated: the development of people to acquire knowledge and soft skills, that is to say, social and financial autonomy.

Until his death in January 2014, Maurice devoted himself to adapted companies, which are real factories that we call UPAI (production, learning, and integration factory). They meet high quality standards and satisfy specific requirements related to the automotive industry. Our operators are all aware of their responsibilities and duties with regard to these requirements. And that, in itself, is an important factor in their progress.

Before leaving us, Maurice left me a note: "Be curious. You can never be curious enough." Plan, organize, control... but there is no point in planning if you don't know how to organize... and there is no point in organizing if you don't know how to control. Always do that while respecting the objectives of the Foundation. "

His work continued by enriching itself with scientific learning and realizations: the plasticity of the brain, now recognized by all; the role of mimetic psychology, interdividuality, and models, all of which are dear to Professor Jean-Michel Oughourlian, through the diligent action of Doctors Pascale Toscani and Pamela Banta-Lavenex, within our Foundation, specifically with their research on cognitive neuroscience and studies on "memories."

France has 600,000 people suffering from various disabilities. They are able to work if they are properly supported and helped. This is our most important challenge. That's what this book is about.

BIBLIOGRAPHY

ALEXANDRE Laurent, La Guerre des intelligences, JC Lattès, 2017.

—, La Mort de la mort, JC Lattès, 2011.

ANSPACH Mark Rogin, À Charge de revanche, les formes élémentaires de la réciprocité, Seuil, coll. La couleur des idées, 2002.

—, Œdipe mimétique, L'Herne, 2010.

ARISTOTE, Poétique, IV, 2, trad. de Marcel Jousse, t. III.

BANDERA Cesareo, Mimesis conflictiva, Madrid, Gredos, 1975.

BATESON Gregory, Steps to an Ecology of Mind, New York, Ballantine Books, 1972.

—, Vers une écologie de l'esprit, Seuil, t. I, 1977 ; t. II, 1980.

BLACKMORE Susan, La Théorie des mêmes, pourquoi nous nous imitons les uns les autres, Max Milo, 2006.

CANETTI Elias, Masse et Puissance, Gallimard, 1966 ; coll. Tel, 1986.

CHERTOK Léon, Le Non-Savoir des psy, Payot, 1979.

CYRULNIK Boris, Sous le signe du lien, Hachette, 1989 ; coll. Pluriel, 1992.

—, avec Patrice Van Eersel, Thierry Janssen, Christophe André, Jean-Michel Oughourlian, Pierre Bustany, Votre cerveau n'a pas fini de vous étonner, Albin Michel, 2012.

DAMASIO Antonio, L'Erreur de Descartes : la raison des émotions, Odile Jacob, 1995.

—, Le Sentiment même de soi : corps, émotions, conscience, Odile Jacob, 1999.

—, Spinoza avait raison : joie et tristesse, le cerveau des émotions, Odile Jacob, 2003.

—, L'Autre moi-même. Les nouvelles cartes du cerveau, de la conscience et des émotions, Odile Jacob, 2010.

DERRIDA Jacques, La Dissémination, Seuil, 1972.

DOSTOÏEVSKI, Crime et Châtiment, trad. André Markowicz, Actes Sud, coll. Thesaurus, 1996.

ELIADE Mircea, Rites and Symbols of Initiation, New York, Harper, 1965.

—, Traité d'histoire des religions, Payot, 1970.

ERICKSON Milton, avec Ernest L. Rossi, L'Intégrale des articles de Milton H. Erickson. T. II : Altération par l'hypnose des processus sensoriels, perceptifs et psychophysiologiques, New York, Irvington, 1980.

FERRY Luc, La Révolution transhumaniste, Plon, 2016.

FREUD Sigmund, Au-delà du principe de plaisir, Payot, 2010.

—, Psychologie de la vie amoureuse, trad. Olivier Mannoni, préface de Robert Neuburger, Payot & Rivages, 2010.

—, Psychologie des foules et analyse du moi, Payot, 2012.

GALLESE Vittorio, Motion, emotion and empathy in esthetic experience (avec David Freedberg), Cognitive sciences, vol. 11, n° 5, 2007.

GANS Eric, The Scenic Imagination. Originary Thinking From Hobbes to the Present Day, Stanford, Stanford University Press, 2008.

—, The Two Sides of Mimesis: Girard's Mimetic Theory, Embodied Simulation and Social Identification, The Journal of Consciousness Studies, 2009.

—, « Intentional attunement: a neurophysiological perspective on social cognition and its disruption in autism », Brain Research, n° 1079, 2006, p. 15-24.

—, Embodied simulation: from neurons to phenomenal experience », Phenomenology and the Cognitive Sciences, n° 4, 2005, p. 23-48.

—, « The manifold nature of interpersonal relations: the quest for a common mechanism », Philosophical Transactions of the Royal Society of London, n° B 358, 2003, p. 517-528.

—, The shared manifold hypothesis: from neurons to empathy, Journal of Consciousness Studies, n° 8 (5-7), 2001, p. 33-50.

GARRELS Scott, Imitation, Mirror Neurons, and Mimetic Desire, Contagion, vol. 12-13, 2006, p. 47-86.

—, Mimesis and Science: Empirical Research on Imitation and the Mimetic Theory of Culture and Religion, East Lansing, Michigan State University Press, 2011.

GIRARD René, Anorexie et Désir mimétique, Paris, L'Herne, 2008.

—, Les Origines de la culture, Hachette Littératures, coll. Pluriel, 2006.

—, La Violence et le Sacré, Grasset, 1972 ; Livre de Poche, 1998.

—, Les Feux de l'envie, William Shakespeare, Grasset, 1990.

—, Mensonge romantique et vérité romanesque, Grasset, 1961; Hachette, coll. Pluriel, 1999.

—, Achever Clausewitz, entretiens avec Benoît Chantre, Champs-Flammarion, 2010.

—, La Conversion de l'art, textes rassemblés par Benoit Chantre et Trevor Cribben Merrill, Champs-Flammarion, 2010.

GOLEMAN Daniel, L'Intelligence émotionnelle, trad. Thierry Piélat, J'ai lu, 2003.

—, Cultiver l'intelligence relationnelle, Paris, Robert Laffont, 2009.

GUILLAUME Paul, L'Imitation chez l'enfant, Félix Alcan, 1926 ; PUF, 1969.

HART L. Sybil et LEGERSTEE, Maria (Eds.), Handbook of Jealousy: Theory, Research, and Multidisciplinary Approaches, Hoboken : Wiley-Blackwell, 2010.

HARARI Yuval Noah, Homo Deus, une brève histoire de l'avenir, Albin Michel, 2017.

KEUKELAERE Simon de, Des découvertes révolutionnaires en sciences cognitives, les paradoxes et dangers de l'imitation, Automates intelligents, n° 63, 2005.

—, La violence humaine : imitation ou mèmes ? Critique d'un point de vue girardien, Automates intelligents, 2002.

LE BON Gustave, Psychologie des foules (1895), PUF, 1963 ; nouvelle édition, 2003.

LE DOUX Joseph, Le Cerveau des émotions, Odile Jacob, 2005.

Maloney Clarence ed., The Evil Eye, New York, Columbia University Press, 1976.

MELTZOFF Andrew, What imitation tells us about social cognition: a rapprochement between developmental psychology and cognitive neuroscience » (avec Jean Decety), Philosophical Transactions of the Royal Society of London, Biologic Sciences, n° 358, 2003.

—, avec Moore, M.K., Imitation of Facial and Manual Gestures by Human Neonates, Science, 198, 75-78, 1977.

—, avec Alison Gopnik, Words, thoughts, and theories, MIT Press, 1997.

—, Elements of a developmental theory of imitation, The Imitative Mind: Development, Evolution and Brain Bases, Cambridge University Press, 2002, p. 19-41.

—, Out of the Mouths of Babes : Imitation, Gaze, and Intentions in Infant Research – the "Like Me" Framework, in S. Garrels, Mimesis and Science : Empirical Research on

Imitation and the Mimetic Theory of Culture and Religion, East Lansing, Michigan State University Press, 2011.

MERRILL Trevor Cribben, The Book of Imitation and Desire: Reading Milan Kundera with René Girard, Bloomsbury, 2013.

—, The Labyrinth of Values: Triangular Desire in Milan Kundera's Dr. Havel after Twenty Years, Heliopolis, Culture Civiltà Politica, Anno VIII, n° 1, Naples, Scripta Web, 2010.

—, The Neurology of Self-Awareness, Edge magazine, Jan. 8, 2007.

RICOEUR Paul, Philosophie de la volonté – II – Finitude et culpabilité, Aubier, 1960-1988.

RIZZOLATI Giacomo et Corrado Sinigaglia, Les Neurones miroirs, traduction Marilène Raiola, Odile Jacob, 2008

—, avec Leonardo Fogassi, Vittorio Gallese, Les neurones miroirs, Pour la science, n° 351, janvier 2007.

—, avec Laila Craighero, The mirror neuron system, Annu. Review neurosciences, n° 27, 2004, p. 169-192.

—, I know what you are doing: a neurophysiological study, Neuron, n° 32, 2001, p. 91-101.

—, avec L. Fogassi, V. Gallese, « Neurophysiological mechanisms underlying the understanding and imitation of action, Nat. Neurosciences review, n° 2, 2001, p. 661-670.

—, avec Michael Arbib, Language within our grasp, Trends in Neurosciences, n° 21, 1998, p. 188-194.

ROUSTANG François, Un destin si funeste, éditions de Minuit, 1977.

—, avec Pierre Babin, Le Thérapeute et son patient, L'Aube, 2000.

SCHELER Max, Nature et formes de la sympathie, Payot et Rivages, 2003.

TARDE Gabriel, Les Lois de l'imitation, Alcan, 1895.

TREVARTHEN Colwyn, Kokkinaki Theano et Fiamenghi jr. Geraldo, What infants' imitations communicate: with mothers, with fathers, with peers. Imitation in Infancy (ed. J. Nadel and G. Butterworth), Cambridge University Press, 1999 ; Wolschlager and Bekkering, 2002.

VEGA Lope de, Le Chien du jardinier, trad. Frédéric Serralta, Gallimard, coll. Folio Théâtre, 2011.

WATZLAWICK Paul, BEAVIN Janet, JACKSON Don, Pragmatics of Human Communication, New York, Norton, 1967. Traduction française, Une logique de la communication, Seuil, 1972.

DEWHURST K., Thomas Willis as a Physician, Los Angeles, University of California Press, 1964.

ACKNOWLEDGEMENTS

I would like to sincerely thank my friend Djénane Kareh Tager who was the linchpin of this book.

Throughout my research, in this book as in the previous ones, I have been inspired and enlightened by the thought of my master and model, René Girard.

I would like to thank very warmly the entire AMIPI team for their welcome as well as for their interest in my work.

FROM THE SAME AUTHOR

- Things Hidden Since the Foundation of the World. Research undertaken with René Girard and Guy Lefort. Translated by Stephen Bann and Michael Metteer, Stanford University Press, 1987.

- The Puppet of Desire: The Psychology of Hysteria, Possession and Hypnosis. Translated by Eugene Webb, Stanford University Press, 1991.

- The genesis of desire. Translated by Eugene Webb, Michigan State University Press, 2009.

- Psychopolitics: Conversations with Trevor Cribben Merrill. Preface by René Girard. Translated by Trevor Cribben Merrill, Michigan State University Press, 2012.

- The Mimetic Brain. Translated by Trevor Cribben Merrill, Michigan State University Press, 2016.

- Alterity. Translated by Andrew J. McKenna, Michigan State University press, 2023.

- Psychiatrie en pratique médicale courante, avec L. Crocq, J.-J. Cottereau et H. Masquin, La Gazette Médicale de France, 1972.

- La Personne du toxicomane, Privat, 1974.

- Approche psychosomatique de la pratique médicale et chirurgicale, avec J.-M. Coldefy, Privat, 1975.

- Le Désir : Énergie et finalité, L'Harmattan, 1995.

- Votre cerveau n'a pas fini de vous étonner (collectif), Albin Michel, 2012.

- Cet autre qui m'obsède. Comment éviter les pièges du désir mimétique, Albin Michel, 2017.

- Optimisez votre cerveau. Neurones miroirs : le mode d'emploi, Plon, 2019.